UNITY

The Power of the
Animal Kingdom
to
Guide You Home

Madeleine Walker

A CIP catalogue record for this book is available from
the British Library.
First Edition 2017

ISBN 978-0-9930376-3-4

Art: Nori Neumann

Formatter/Editor: Corrina Thorby

Publisher: Lynn Morris

To my grandson Theo,
the boy with the ocean eyes

Endorsements

'In her new book, Unity: The Power of the Animal Kingdom to Guide You Home, author and animal communicator, Madeleine Walker includes us in her extraordinary encounters with wild and domestic animals and the healing to be found at sacred places on earth. She shares with the reader unique techniques for changing current reality, healing ourselves and our animals, re-visioning past lives, and healing the earth - arcane knowledge that is needed by all, now more than ever before'.

Marta Williams
Biologist, animal communicator and author of:
My Animal My Self and Learning Their Language
www.martawilliams.com

'Do you ever sit and ask what exactly is going wrong with the world right now? Is there nothing I can do to change things? You can do, if you can just get your head around the fact that we are all human, animal, fish, mammal, insect, bird, bat – all linked, and not only that, but if you follow the teaching of the amazing Madeleine Walker, you will discover that we are all interchangeable. The flow of energy throughout all our species makes us an inextricable part of the whole, and if we chose we can adjust our energy to become a different part of the whole, to understand nature, really and fully, and allow ourselves to become greater than the sum of the parts of every creature on Earth. We can change and heal past traumas and free ourselves. Is this making your brain hurt? Fear not, follow Madeleine on her incredible global journeys and find all the answers you need to vastly expand your horizons. Her understanding of universal living things has grown over the past 15 years that I have known her, so that now she simply glows with it. In this book, she shares all of that with you, so that you too can

glow, and become a being that can change things, and can heal the planet, not with wishy-washy 'green' stuff, but with a transformed mind and spirit'.
Jenny Smedley
Bestselling author of 25 books including:
Pets Have Souls Too, and The Tree That Talked
www. jennysmedley.co.uk

'Mystics since the dawn of humanity have told us that everything is one, and that we are never truly alone. Science tells us that everything is energy, and our bodies contain the constituents of stars. In this extraordinary book Madeleine Walker weaves together past, present and future through her communications with animals and their people. She describes how all creatures are our guides and teachers, and how we can use this healing wisdom to transform negative energy to positive. When we learn to listen and to connect with animals as portals to insight and wisdom, deep transformation is possible'.
Lisa Tenzin-Dolma
Principal of the International School for Canine Psychology & Behaviour and author of 33 books, including: Charlie, the Dog Who Came in from the Wild
www.theiscp.com

"Unity" is rich with insight into the world of the non-human beings who share this beautiful planet with us. Now more than any time in human history it is critical for us to wake up and tune into this extraordinary wisdom. Madeleine is the real deal, dive into this practical, enlighten-ing and inspiring book, you will be transformed!'
Dr Linda Bender
Author of: Animal Wisdom - Learning from the Spiritual Lives of Animals
www.lindabender.org

Preface

Gifts from the Guardians of Gaia

The animal kingdom wants and *needs* us to be healed - to be all that we are - to remember our magnificence!

The lions wish us to be lion hearted. The whale nation wishes us to only feel love - the dolphins want us to be in - joy! Our domestic pets are with us to guide us on our path of day to day challenge, to work through our emotional and physical issues that we have chosen to create. To find our way home through the struggles of a 3-dimensional experience, to expand our awareness into the new paradigm of the 4th dimension and above.

None of us like to feel alone, separate or isolated. We all crave to feel that we belong and that we're a part of some-thing big and important, that there's a reason why we're here, that there has to be some meaning to it all!

This book is indeed for everyone who may feel disconnected from themselves, weighed down with baggage and negative mind-sets. For those who may feel lost, unforgiven and unfulfilled, without remembering their soul purpose and who dream of a simpler more empowered life. We need to be in tune with and wake up to the magic of nature, the wisdom of animals and a remembering of their ancient wisdom and skills. There is a great need to feel a true sense of community and to find harmony as co-creators with all living things.

We need to wake up and remember that we have every-thing inside of us, stored deep within our DNA to achieve this... we just need to be shown how!

The book illustrates how the author spent many years working with animals and their humans, bridging the gap of understanding between them. The purpose and mission of this book is to raise awareness and recognition of the vital importance of the animal kingdom and nature for the future of humankind.

'The more the animals have taught me, the more I realise just how important they are to our future and that of our planet. I started to wonder if wild species also wanted to help us re-connect to ourselves and our beautiful Mother Earth as well! This has set me on the path of incredible journeys, travelling far and wide, intuiting messages and getting up close and sometimes scarily personal, with some very large wild creatures, who have blessed me with their wisdom and grace. I have also reconnected with wonderful indigenous elders, who still retain the knowledge and wisdom of our ancestral links to nature and the animal kingdom. The animals feel no separation from this our Earth. Their wisdom reminds us that we are all one. They wish for a collective reunion … an interspecies unification. This book records the messages from some incredible sources; this has become my mission, obsession and passion to share, so that we can reconnect with our beloved earth and ultimately with ourselves, in order to bring us home. The animals have helped me to reclaim my power, remember who I am and why I am here. It is to be the voice of truth for the animals, who have shared their healing techniques and guiding love, so that I may be healed, but also that I am now able to share and facilitate profound healing for my fellow humans.'

The book shows us that we are all so much more than we think we are - we can learn wisdom from the humble house fly, to the humpback whale - they all have a voice and they all want us to listen, learn and **WAKE UP**. The animal wisdom in this book shows you how!!

Contents

loss of their family pets, only to realise that these pets were their human family in past lives! This helps you understand that you can feel just as traumatised when your pet passes, as any human loss, as they are indeed 'family' or maybe I should say furmily!!

Chapter 3

Creating a safe place to conceive - re-write the past to change a traumatic pregnancy or birth experience.

Case studies where animals have led their owners back to past lives, where there has been trauma connected to their pregnancies and situations where it has been very unsafe to have a child. These traumas are stored at a cellular level and can prevent people conceiving and having the child that they've always wanted in their current life. When the animals take you back to those times, you can heal those memories and this chapter shows how miracles can happen when you can change your DNA memory - thanks to the wisdom of your pets and some-times slightly larger animals!

Chapter 4
Overcome your self-limiting fear and pain with a little help from your furry friends

Cases where human and animal fear and pain are ruining their lives and when we delve a little deeper we can find out why and change them into confidence. Reclaim your magnificence!

Chapter 5
Forgive yourself! Cetacean soul healing

The wild Egyptian spinner dolphins show you how you can erase parasitic (guilt) energies within your DNA from eons ago and become whole again. They also teach you how to journey back to work with etheric light crystals and perform transformative body scans.

PART 2

PLANETARY HEALING...
Gifts from the guardians of Gaia

Chapter 6
Walking between worlds.... Meet the Ancestors

A very unexpected visitor gives us strange messages from a very unusual source. Planetary healing in Uluru using light crystals, reconnecting us with our co-guardianship of our planet. How to work with light crystals.

Chapter 7
Where Whales and Lions meet a shamanic home coming

Beautiful messages from blue and grey whales align with the white lions. Sperm whales reconnect with the Kalahari Bushmen, unifying through sound and ancient ancestral wisdom with deep connections with nature. This chapter allows you to see the 'bigger picture' of unification.

Chapter 8
Water Wisdom

Information from the whales about data stored in the molecular memory of water, which can affect your physical skeletal structures, whether you have a puddle or a pond, a lake or an ocean, you can still give healing to yourself and our 'blue' planet.

Chapter 9
The return of Nagwal and the healing whales of Tonga

Adventures in Vava'u, swimming with more humpbacks, being blissed out with the most incredible encounters and life changing downloads to share with you all.

Chapter 10
Meditations from the Guardians of Gaia to heal yourselves and the earth

Beautiful healing meditations sharing the techniques gifted to me from many incredible sources.

The white whale energy teaches you how to release fear and embrace love, whilst uniting to heal our earth. Meet the guardians who are showing themselves more and more now to assist us. Get up close and personal with your healing allies - Dragons, Dolphins, Inner Earth beings, Unicorns and many more!

Conclusion

How can you find Unity?

Acknowledgements

Resources

Bibliography

About the Author

Introduction

Unity
Interspecies Unification

Have you ever wondered why your pet seems to just stare at you? Has it made you think that you know he or she is trying to tell you *something*, but you're not sure just what! Well I can tell you that they definitely *are* trying to let you know that they understand *so* much more than you might have thought! My life's journey up to now has had its fair share of ups and downs - lots of downs I had thought, but now I realise how perfect they were to lead me to this very moment in time, so that I can now share my adventure, learning from the animals.

My pets were always my constant in an ever changing world - they never seemed to let me down or forsake me for another! I have always been crazy about animals and thanks to the patience and love from my mother; we always had a real menagerie in my childhood home! All they did was shower me with their love and just be there! The only sadness they brought me was when they had to pass with their all too short lifespans. But I now know that even this grief can be eased and healed from their continued support from spirit and the promise that we all meet up again, and that nothing and no-one is ever truly lost. They have shown me on so many occasions that we all travel together in our soul families, through many lifetimes. More than this though, they have mentored me into being their messenger, having tutored me in some quite ground-breaking healing techniques. They have expanded my life beyond all recognition and I am eternally grateful to them. They have led me from a shy stay at home single mum that was living on a shoestring, to an international speaker, author and consultant, loving every minute of my work, revelling in my adventure and further tuition from the animals and the wonderful people that I meet and help along the way.

The very first animal to 'talk' to me was a little Jack Russell puppy called Sam. Not only was it a shock to hear his voice in my head, but his message was what really blew me away. He 'told' me that he was a reincarnation of his owner's old dog and that he had decided to come back now, to help her through a tough time in her life! He then proceeded to 'morph' into the old dog, to show me what he looked like in that previous incarnation, so that I could describe his information to his owner - as you can imagine I was rather nervous at sharing this, but an old photo of the previous dog confirmed exactly what the puppy had shown me, and the owner admitted that even though they had only been together for five days, she felt that the little pup just *knew* her every move and mood. So although this was a completely new concept for us, she found it totally acceptable, as she had realised that they had such an instant profound connection with each other when they first met. This was quite a revelation for all of us and certainly opened up my awareness in so many ways. That one little pup was the catalyst to get me to where I am today, right here, sharing what has become my life's mission, with you!

As you will discover, your animals can help you completely change your mind-set, in order to help you create the life you are worthy of, deserving the very best. However more than that, they want you to awaken to the concept that we need to come together, to unify, in order to move forwards on all levels to help the animals help us, to heal the planet.

The dictionaries define the word Unity as *a state of forming a complete and harmonious whole, the state or quality of being one; oneness, the act, state, or quality of forming a whole from separate parts, something whole or complete that is composed of separate parts, mutual agreement; harmony or concord.*

The following chapters describe messages from some very unusual sources, who wish to convey their desire for unity between the formerly separate 'parts' of humankind and the animal kingdom. The more I have connected with animals and nature, the more I have been convinced by them of the importance of this coming together into a state of harmony and 'oneness'.

I am constantly amazed at their willingness to educate and remind us of our soul connections with our beloved earth, and that unless we do wake up and remember our connections, there is little hope for our future, as we continue to desecrate and decimate the beauty and bounty of Mother Earth. As an animal communicator and human empowerment coach, the animals have taught me everything I know, as they have shown me healing techniques to help humans and animals understand their deep connections and release traumas through many shared lifetimes. I have travelled extensively to find answers and physically connect with many wild species in their natural environments, so that they can choose with free will, to interact and guide me. I feel so humbled by their generosity and trust in allowing me to come into close contact with them and on occasion, their young.

The overwhelming message seems to be one of re-empowerment of remembering whom and what we humans are, how *we* are all one. Anyone who believes that we are separated from the animals by our concepts of love and emotions has never seen the way an elephant mother nurtures her calf, or honours a fallen herd member. Perhaps they've never seen a gorilla caress its baby, or the way lion pride members greet each other with such fondness and reverence. I have also felt the depth of love shown to a human by an animal and anyone who has felt that love, knows that it is given unconditionally. I have been given the task of raising awareness of this coming together, and its importance at this

Time of a new paradigm of spiritual awareness and awakening, by the animals. It is a great responsibility, but a duty I willingly perform as some kind of recompense for all the blessings the animals have given me.

We have to remember that we are so multi-dimensional and there is *so* much more than our limited 3D perspective. Many times I have felt the presence of spirit animals and ancestors guiding me forwards and backwards in time, into other dimensions and the following chapters relay some of those experiences.

Part One of the book, you will read amazing case studies of life changing healing from our pets, who know exactly what we need to do in order to heal and release our self-limiting beliefs. You will learn about past life script re-writing, changing your pre-birth soul contracts and many more techniques to free yourself from constricting disempowerment and how to reclaim your magnificence! **Part Two** is about the adventure and journey that the animals have led me on to teach me how to heal myself, other human beings, and ultimately our beautiful planet! To look deep into the eye of a whale as it gazes back at you with such compassion. To feel the ice blue stare of a white lion bore into your very soul as it approaches you, these are just some of the wonders that await your discovery as I describe just how that feels in this book!

When we learn to SPEAK with the animals

To LISTEN with animal ears and

SEE through animal eyes

We experience the phenomena, the power,

The potential of the human essence.

Ted Andrews
Animal Speak

'Our task must be to free ourselves from this prison
by widening our circle of compassion to embrace
all living creatures and the whole of nature
in it's beauty'

Albert Einstein

PART 1

PERSONAL HEALING
with animals...we are ALL ONE

Chapter 1

Renew Your Contract!

This chapter introduces the concept that we are all inextricably linked and that we can have many lifetimes together in many different guises as animals *and* humans, depending on our soul journey. I believe that humans are *not* the superior species - what better way to show unconditional love than by reincarnating as a dog! Choosing to incarnate as an animal allows us to be so open and uncluttered by our human egos, which definitely get in the way of unlocking our awareness to the group consciousness, which is available to us all if we let it! The animals choose to remind us of our connection, we just have to listen to them!

We are all so deeply connected - the animals know this and are so committed to waking us up to remembering and reclaiming our strengths and life purpose, which is to heal ourselves and our beloved planet. It isn't always appropriate to delve into past lives, as some of the issues impacting on you can be very current, but you can still use the following techniques to resolve self-limiting beliefs and create a better future for yourself.

Your animals will know exactly what needs to be done for your highest good and fulfilment of your potential.

"I must have been mad to agree to sign up to this!" I don't know about you but I've said this to myself many times, when people have told me that we all have an agreed plan or contract of our incarnations, and the challenges we create to resolve unfinished business from the past. My belief is that we can change our past and that we can also change our past and that we can also change our current realities, by literally changing our thinking with a little help from the animals!

They have told me that we have a pre-birth meeting with our soul family as energy forms, (human and animal) and decide, always from a place of love, how we are all going to interact for our greatest learning and soul growth. The animals have taught me that they play such a huge part in our learning, and commit to helping us in the best way they can, sometimes enduring great suffering themselves, in order to relieve our deepest pain. I am constantly humbled by their selflessness and yearning to bring us home to ourselves. I am being given an image of the little Jack Russell sitting next to the gramophone player for the old picture of 'His Master's Voice', but this time it's like the dog has a megaphone, shouting out "Wake up, remember what you're here for. You can do it - go for it!" These Jack Russell pups know a thing or two!

As a child you may have retained memories of your past lives and your life's mission this time around. Unfortunately once you start to grow up, you can forget what you came here to do, and so you may struggle along in the dark, stumbling through your challenges until something forces you to say "Enough already!" Then you can find ways as to how you might find resolution for your emotional or physical issues. I feel that your pasts, both in this life and other incarnations, shape who you are today and once you understand why you have fear and self-limiting challenges, and where they come from, they lose their power over you, and are easily resolved. It's when they remain unexplained that they may continue to have a hold and restrict your potential happiness and present fulfilment. This is what happened to me and if I can change it, so can you! I definitely felt it was time to rewrite my past and rethink my contract! Surely there had to be more to life than this? Fortunately with the help of a very special horse and a cat, I found out how! This next story was to be the start of learning to use a wonderful technique that has changed so many people's lives that I've worked with. I am eternally grateful to such a wise special creature that came into my life just at the right time to help me upgrade my healing methods!

Jess the happy ending horse

When visiting and working with a beautiful horse called Jess and her owner one day, we had opened up a whole can of worms in a very traumatic past life. The horse had become so jealous of the owner's other horses in her curent incarnation, and seemed to be in a state of utter terror, whenever they went through narrow paths with overhanging rocks or vegetation. Her wide eyes seemed just to be permanently in a state of 'red alert'. Jess showed me telepathically, in a kind of video clip in my mind, a time when her current owner was a male gold prospector; leading his horses as pack animals behind him through a rocky pass, with Jess taking up the rear. Unfortunately a huge cougar leapt down on Jess, breaking her back, whilst the other horses bolted in fear carrying Jess' owner away before he could help. Jess' dying thoughts were of abandonment and fear. Amazingly the horses she was so jealous of now, were the same ones in that previous life - they had all come together to heal this awful past. Clear as day Jess said to me "Can't we just have a happy ending?" The owner was suddenly feeling a huge sense of heaviness and guilt in her heart, the intensity of which really surprised her in this unexpected direction the session was taking (she had never experienced any kind of regression before). I asked Jess to help us resolve this combined trauma between them. I thought changing the ending was a great idea, but I wasn't quite sure how we could! The horse showed me an alternative safe and happy ending and suggested guiding her owner through this different scenario, really absorbing the new qualities of safety, security and most importantly of all... love. I was guided to ask the owner to visualize herself as the director of her life movie and to decide to change the movie's ending and create a much happier scene! The owner commenced to describe just using her imagination, exactly what the horse had shown me, without me telling her! The owner could describe exactly what she was wearing as that man, and every detail of what the horses looked like in that lifetime, which was not as they appeared now. I was amazed at what was happening, as Jess became very calm and her eyes had softened and were totally focused on showing us what we had to do next. The owner said that she was visualizing the prospector seeing the cougar just in time to fire a warning shot to scare it away, so they could all be safe and then getting to their destination safely. The prospector was thanking the horses for carrying his possessions to a place where they could rest. I felt guided to ask her to really absorb the feelings of safety and security and love for her horses, which she did, saying that the awful weight in her chest had miraculously lifted and she felt suddenly so much more at peace with herself, with a huge sense of relief now. I then felt, guided by Jess, to ask her owner to follow a timeline into the future, where she saw the horses living out a safe and happy life until a natural end came for them, having many happy years together. So much love emanated from Jess at this point, that we both felt really emotional and it felt like all the horses in the barn gave a huge sigh of something being released. I felt that they had now brought back as a cellular memory, only feelings of love and safety, which could now impact in a positive healing way on them all. I was thrilled to find out that almost immediately after our session, Jess had become really calm when ridden and no longer tried to attack the other horses in her previous fits of jealousy if her owner spent any time with them. Her owner also felt much happier in herself, as though she had been carrying a great weight and a sense of failure, without knowing why, but was amazed at the difference she felt in her levels of confidence and abilities to cope with her life challenges. I now feel that we can create a new dimension where the trauma never occurred, so that we can store those new realities in our DNA. Russian scientists including biophysicist and molecular biologist Pjotr Garjajev and his colleagues, also explored the vibrational behaviour of DNA. They have found that 90% of our so called 'junk' DNA can be reprogrammed by sound vibration and thought frequencies.

Our DNA can contain all these memories and traumas from our lifetimes that we call past lives, but are actually running consecutively and that we can also dip in and out of these life memories to heal trauma, but also reclaim special gifts and skills that we may have forgotten in the current life. How fortunate that animals seem to want to help us heal these memories in order to be empowered and whole once more. The animals seem to be 'hotwired' into the group consciousness of what they call the 'All', so they know exactly how to access this information and luckily for us they want to share it with us!

Cindy the cat, contract consultant!

The next 'upgrade' came from another unexpected source… a very clever cat! I love to offer people distant readings for themselves and their animals if they are unable to visit me for a consultation. I always marvel at the animals' ability to 'flag up' issues that need addressing in their owners and these 'issues' are usually the cause of some possible bad behaviour or the physical problems from the animal, which is why their owners call

6

on my help - little do they know what the animals have in store for *them*! I received a letter from a person called Celia, which contained a lovely photograph of herself - a slightly more mature lady in very conventional twin set and pearls attire, cuddling a lovely black and white cat called Cindy. As I read through the words describing why she was requesting a reading for Cindy, I began to intuit some very strange and unsettling images that Cindy was telepathically showing me. I decided to telephone Celia and discuss my visions. What unfolded left me quite in-credulous. Poor Celia had been having a terrible time. In the past she had been sexually assaulted, stalked, burgled and in so many ways totally disempowered. This had quite understandably left her frightened to leave her house, but also frightened to stay in it. She was wary of everyone and always feared the worst in any situation. She was ruled by her fear and sadly was creating more negative situations because of her belief in a cruel and unsafe world. I have learnt now not to dismiss the messages from animals, however strange they might appear - there have been many times I have doubted my sanity, and wondered how on earth I might relay the weird and seemingly fantastic messages coming through from a little furry friend! This case was no exception! Cindy began to show me images, like a video clip of an era that she told me was Atlantis, and of an attack of very negative looking beings. By this time I thought I was beginning to lose the plot and wondered how on earth I was going to mention these 'small' details! However I had underestimated Celia's openness to these concepts, as she admitted, quite freely in a matter of fact way, that she had always been fascinated by the idea of Atlantis and could picture herself there very easily, when I asked Cindy to 'show' us. I always ask an animal to telepathically show me a scenario and then without describing any detail, I ask the person to tell me what they can 'see' as their animal guides us to gain deeper

7

understanding of the root cause of an issue. As with Jess's owner, when they can relate exactly what I've been seeing and hearing from the animal, I know we're all on the same page and that we can get to work! However, after Celia had read the following letter from me, Cindy decided that we both needed some further tuition in *really* creating a better life for ourselves!

Dear Celia

Herewith some information from Cindy

Grounding and transmuting

I always ask for a word or phrase that underpins the whole reading and this is what I get from Cindy.

As we know she has been working very hard to allow you to access the memory that brought you to this place in your current life. She has so committed to being your protector, but you have lost sight of the importance of her role as you have with yours. I feel that you do have this contract to experience the human challenges and because you have lost sight of your work here that Cindy has been trying to remind you of, as she is part of this contract, everything has got out of hand. You might think why on earth would I agree to do this??? But on a deep soul level there is a very important reason. You would have agreed to live a human life with all its ups and downs, bringing your own special energy to healing some dark energies on the planet. This will probably sound completely mad to an outsider – all I can say that in my work I have come to expect the unexpected. Cindy just gave me some insight into something you said about this man putting something in you? I'm getting that it was a memory of an object that was implanted. I've removed several of these from people, horses and dogs. They are most unpleasant and I feel this again is just replaying something from the past. I'm getting a very negative energy and it's most unpleasant! You have to remember that you and Cindy - but especially you - are an enormous force - an immense being! You have just got very bogged down in this human experience and completely given your power away and become a bit of a victim! It's very symbolic that Cindy has the arthritis in her paws as anything to do with the legs and feet is always to do with a block in taking the next step forward. She feels your complete block and fear of 'what next'! Of course things happen to other people, like burglaries, but I do feel that by being so anxious about any caller (quite understandably!!) you are in a mind-set now of expecting the worst and perpetuating these very strange happenings! I feel it's time to say enough now! I've learnt what I had to; I want to be able to enjoy my human life in peace now. I feel we need to go back to the past life where the original negative experience happened and re-write some rules! I hope this doesn't sound too weird!

During our phone call as it progressed, I felt Cindy start to give directions as to how to change the whole past attack in Atlantis, where there was reconciliation and a unifying of forces transmuting the dark into light. This seemed to resolve easily, but then Cindy said we could also try another method to change the present time and also create a far happier future! She telepathically talked us through just how to do this, when she showed Celia an image of a large board room with a huge oval table. There were several 'beings' sitting around the table with what looked like scrolls and folders in front of them. She then guided Celia to see if she could recognise any of the other participants in this meeting, and she sensed the presence of the man who had attacked her in this life. Far from feeling scared of this interaction she realised that it was a very loving meeting, and that all concerned were focussed on creating the greatest soul growth, as they decided who and how they were going to 'play out' their next lifetime together. Cindy said this was all well and good, but that it was time now for Celia to choose what she wanted from *now* on in her incarnation. Cindy said she had to visualise her 'contract' and imagine writing exactly what she wanted now with the most beautiful feather quill, dipped in very special ink. She was advised to think very carefully when she was writing, and that everything had to be written in the present tense, as though it was happening *now*. Celia said that she wrote things like "I now choose to know that I am safe in my life etc..." She could 'see' it all so clearly, as she could almost hear the sound of the feather nib scratching the new clauses in her life from now on!

Cindy then instructed her to imagine old fashioned wax to seal the document, so that it was literally 'signed and sealed'. She had to imagine pressing her unique seal, like a ring or a stamp to close the deal! I asked her what her seal was, and she said it looked like a beautiful dove in flight, which I thought was very symbolic of the new peace and freedom she was now choosing in her life! As you will read, I have used this technique to great effect many times, as it seems to anchor into your reality the total commitment of intent to choose only the most positive and gentle healing realities, in the future. Cindy seemed very happy with our work, as Celia having been sitting on her lap for the entire call, Cindy had obviously dismissed us from class then, as she just jumped down and sauntered off looking very pleased with herself!

Cindy's board meeting helps again

Pat had asked me to help her with her dog and we resolved some really amazing past life issues between them, which had really created a fantastic deepening of their relationship. However Pat still felt that she was giving her power away and allowing herself to be continually controlled by an ex-partner. He seemed to be actually dictating and orchestrating her every move and preventing her from moving forward in her life, having under-mined her confidence to cope on her own. She was a very strong woman, but had forgotten that she had everything within her to create whatever she wanted, an empowered non-dependant individual. Cindy and Pat's dog worked with her during a skype session that we had, to 'fine tune' Pat's future! Pat visualised the board room table covered in files all in a messy jumble, with no order. She sensed her dominating parents there and most definitely her 'ex'!

So following Cindy's procedure, Pat unravelled her life scroll, and dipping the pen in the ink constructed exactly what she wanted to create in her life *now*. After writing her new clause, she was amazed when she looked around the room, as the previously scattered files on the table, were all neatly stacked with hers on the top! We felt that all the other files from the people who had challenged her most, were absorbing and 'downloading' the new clauses into their database, so that their future interactions with Pat would understand the new 'rules'! Pat contacted me a couple of weeks later, and said that she couldn't believe how laid-back her previous partner had now become - allowing her to make the new decisions in her life, and accepting that he didn't have any right to try and influence her to his advantage anymore! Even her parents seemed much more accepting of Pat's beliefs and were far more supportive of her new directions that she wanted to expand on.

So if you want to work with Cindy's technique and reclaim your magnificence, living your life through joy instead of struggle, think about what you would write at your pre-birth meeting. This is so that you can only choose loving, fulfilling experiences, having learnt what you needed for your best and highest soul growth. What about... "I now choose love, abundance, security, limit-less opportunities for my fulfilment! Etc... Etc..." Reclaim whatever you want, deserve and are worthy of receiving right now. You may be able to read the previous memos in your file, scroll, or whatever you can imagine, as to why you had to go through any tough times. You can also dialogue with your soul family to see if they can also guide you further in understanding your life path. Once understanding why and you finally 'get it', you can then move on! This is so much better than struggling on in the dark, blindly repeating old patterns of self-limitation and fearful situations. Isn't it wonderful that your animal friends are so happy to guide you into being all that you are!

"Only love, forgiveness and compassion will heal the earth, despite what humankind has done to our species, we only send love. You have become detached from "The All" we send our love to bring you back home"

Message from the cetacean nation.

Chapter 2

Animal Soul Mates…Healing Your Grief

Sadly I know only too well the awful pain that grief can bring. When people talk about heart ache, I know what they mean now. I have felt my heart actually physically hurt with the sense of loss and the deep hole of emptiness inside, when one of my loved ones dies. Many people contact me because they find that they are not coping at all well when their animals die.

Very often they receive little sympathy from family and friends who might say things like "it's only a cat - just get another one!" or "It was only a dumb dog!"

However, I love to try and reassure them by intuiting their connections. Very often animals will show me what their next incarnation will look like and how they might return to their bereaved owners. I have received so much evidence from the animals that their human's grief is very real, but that our souls are eternal and that they are never 'lost'. As I have said, we do travel in soul families and when you seem to have such an incredible bond with your animal, they literally can be your 'soul mate'! I am greatly comforted now to know this and that we do all reconnect through many lifetimes, but of course it's the physical contact of a hug we miss the most! The following incredible case stories will, I hope, help you understand this and you'll never look at your animals in the same way again!

Cats Capuchino and Honey help their human

Keith emailed me to ask if I'd perform a reading for his cat Honey. His other cat Capuchino had died and he was very concerned about losing his other cat Honey, as she seemed so depressed and sad. As you will read.

Honey was doing a great job in flagging up what Keith

needed to heal in himself! He was devastated at the awful death of Capuchino and was really struggling to understand why this had to happen. He told me that he didn't want any kind of stupid platitudes like "well it must have been his time", and "he must have done what he came to do" or "there's a reason for everything". He was so angry at what he called the pointlessness of it all, when Cappy (as he called him) was still so young with his whole life ahead of him, with such a loving home and seemingly everything to live for!

This was the first message I received from Keith;

'One of our beloved cats Capuchino, whom I rescued from a wheelie bin in Spain, was horrifically killed recently in a dog attack. My other cat Honey is exhibiting bizarre symptoms and won't eat. I know she's in grief, as we all are, but she's trying to tell me something and I just don't know what it is. If this continues, she will go into a serious decline. I've tried the vet, but there's nothing wrong physically (yet) so I need your help before it's too late'.

Luckily Keith was open to the concept of re-incarnation, but was almost inconsolable. This is what I intuited from lovely Honey who was also rescued several years earlier in Spain and had lived many happy years in Keith's family home. This then led on to the profound connection with Cappy.

Reading for Keith, Cappy and Honey 25/04.13

Dear Keith

Herewith some information from Honey and Cappy.

I feel that Honey is trying to tell you that she is feeling your grief - I can see why you are so devastated - Cappy was such an extraordinarily beautiful cat. I'm sure you love Honey very much, but she feels as though she is not enough - I feel this goes back to her previous home and separation. When you got

Cappy and he was such a gorgeous kitten, she did feel second best, though I'm sure you tried your best to treat them both as if they were equally loved - it's just some insecurities in Honey's make up - so her not eating is a mixture of a kind of attention seeking, but also grief. She feels very confused as though (this might sound silly) she almost feels guilty that she has you to herself once again now, but at the same time does miss Cappy and of course hates to feel the pain that you're going through. So perhaps you can try talking to her as though you understand her confusion and sadness - tell her that she is enough and has always been enough, it's just that you wanted to help other cats as well and to share your love with them too. This might sound as though I'm humanising Honey emotionally, but as I said we have to remember that these are huge sentient beings with very strong emotions too! Try talking it over with her either in your mind or verbally and see how she responds - very often just being 'heard' can really help and also there is a wonderful homeopathic remedy for grief called Ignatia 1M which can really help you cope a little better.

Healing and Monitoring

I always ask for a word or phrase to underpin a reading and this is what I get for you and Honey

I feel that Honey was just left and found her way to the villa where she 'found' you. It might seem like a strange thing to say, but I feel somehow Honey helped you find yourself? I feel she opened up a part of your heart that you had closed down - maybe through grief of loss of a loved one or pain from a previous relationship - or maybe both? I'm being told that Honey seemed to make sense of your life once again, almost like she made you have faith in good things happening again? Not quite sure what she's telling me, but I'm sure you can tell me! I do feel she was quite well looked after by a couple, but that they had some money worries which created relationship problems and so they had to leave, which was all orchestrated

15

then come to you and commence her healing with you! I feel this is why she has a special place in your heart. I also feel there's something about enhancing your relationship with your partner?

I'm not sure how she would respond to having a new kitten - at the moment it feels a bit too raw still and might reinforce her perception of not being enough. Also I feel there's more healing for you to do from Cappy. Ofcourse it would be nice if she could have some company when you do have to be away, but you can overcome this my 'talking' to her when you are away so that she can feel into your energy.

I apologise if this is a little personal, but have you suffered from depression in the past at all? I feel Honey has been such a good therapist for this and one of the reasons that she's so clingy now, is that she is worried about your emotional health, with losing Cappy, as it doesn't seem to make any sense and has brought up all the old feelings of it being just a 'cruel senseless world' again? When she is with you she can monitor your energy and although you're bound to be very sad - at least she can see the extent of your grief - when you're away she can only guess and feels powerless to be of help, as she has been so wonderfully in the past by just being close to you. By telepathically talking to her when you have to be away, she will be able to link in with you much better.

This really does work as I had to do it with my old Border terrier when I was working away, as she would fret and then sulk when I got home – once I realised that I could connect with her at any time when I was away, she was fine! So as I suggested before, keep 'talking' to Honey and I'm sure it will help. She has chosen to be your guardian and to help you through this, which is why she 'found' you. She is also very aware of the past life connections and karmic issues around you and Cappy, which is what we will look into now.

Cappy
Grief/Separation/Understanding

I do hope that looking into your past life connections with the being that is Cappy will help you understand the reasons for your reconnection in this lifetime. This has not been a 'test' or a 'punishment', but an expansion of understanding just how deep your connections are with Cappy and that there has to be a learning of the 'bigger picture', which can be so hard to comprehend from our 3D perceived realities. I guess we'll only really know the truth of it when we pass ourselves!

You were so meant to find Cappy and to reconnect with him. He has been telling me about a past life that he shared with you in Russia during the revolution as your son. I'm not sure if you've felt drawn to have children in this lifetime, but I get a sense that you may not have? Or if you have, you may have felt strong reservations about it? I feel that sadly Cappy died at quite a young age - I feel from a stray bullet in an uprising. It feels like he was in the wrong place at the wrong time and created what seemed a completely senseless passing and waste of a young life back then. There's something stored within your DNA about blame and not being able to forgive yourself, which seems to have perpetuated this trauma. I'm certainly not suggesting that his death as a young cat this time is your fault at all! Its Cappy's way of bringing this all to a head in order for it to be finally healed, so that he can come back to you in what-ever form he next chooses for a long and happy life with you. Unfortunately there are painful steps along the way for all of us, as we heal these parts of our journeys that we share together. This is a HUGE, very difficult concept for you to accept I know, and I will be happy to discuss this with you. Sometimes it can be such a brief reconnection, just to set wheels in motion for the next stage of your shared journey together, as I had with my beautiful cat Thebes who was killed at 8 months - to only have 6 months together seemed so cruel, but I understand now exactly why he did this and that he will be coming back when he's ready, he's guided me to do the work I must do now. Believe me when I say it has been incredibly hard for me to accept, even knowing what I know and believe now!

See when you read about your Russian life, whether you get any kind of feelings or images of those times in your mind, if you can picture what Cappy might have looked like as a young boy, try and expand the picture in your mind and see if you can conjure up any images of your life together. If it brings up emotions, visualise changing the whole outcome where you can now see him growing up into adulthood and then maybe looking after you in your old age. Be creative - it might just feel like you're just making the whole thing up or fantasising, but what you can do is to create a whole new dimension, where the trauma never happened, so that you don't have to carry any of the old residue in your DNA any more. This will free you both up to reconnect in much happier times, when he comes back and also help you understand that there is so much more to our 3D realities and that we really can create new ones. I have had great success with human and animal clients by performing this 're-write' of their life scripts, freeing them from past trauma to start anew. I know that many of my animals have been with me before and that those that have passed will be coming back. The cat I have now came straight back after passing, within months - my dogs even recognised him as soon as he walked into the house as a tiny kitten! So I'm sure Cappy will find a way back to you when he's ready. I feel he will come back as a cat again, as it seems to be such a good way to be accepted into your heart! (They say cats leave paw prints on our hearts and it's so true!) I feel you are far more discerning and reserved with your feelings towards humans! I find it much easier to have an open heart towards animals - not so easy with people! I feel this is why the grief has been so unbearable and felt so senseless, as it was bringing up the loss again from the past life as a double 'whammy' making it even more intense.

Let me know your thoughts on this and we can have a chat about it in order to hopefully make some sense for you.

Keith rang me and we had a session together to re-write the past. With Cappy's help from spirit, it was amazing how vivid the visions and emotions of that Russian lifetime were that came flooding into Keith's consciousness. He said that he could picture exactly what Cappy would have looked like his young son. He described his clothes, and I could picture every scene with him against a cold, grey, harsh backdrop of a Russian town during the revolution. The boy had gone out to find some bread, but a violent demonstration had erupted. Keith had gone to find him to get him home to relative safety, but they'd got caught up in the army's retaliation and a stray bullet tragically ended his son's young life. In order to transmute this, I asked Keith how he could completely reframe the whole scenario. He visualised a completely different ending, where they had managed to get to safety, as someone had warned them of the march. Then he 'saw' his son growing up and finding his way, making his own life, and then looking after Keith in his old age and supporting him as he passed over. I asked Keith to really breathe in the sense of relief, safety and the knowledge that he had Kept his son safe and protected, instead of the complete desolation that he'd previously felt. This seemed to allow Keith to process his feelings about the passing of Cappy much better. He fully understood why Cappy had chosen to leave at that time in that way, in order to heal these very deep wounds, stored inside for so long.

Keith also admitted that he'd been very concerned to ever have children, as he had felt that the world was a very cruel place. He had always felt that it was far safer to allow animals into his heart, rather than humans and he had suffered from depression in the past without ever fully understanding where his deep sadness and self-blame came from. He was left with a feeling of immense gratitude for Cappy's commitment to heal him and a sense of a more hopeful future, when Cappy could return to share a long and happy life with him!

More grieving cats!
Janine and Bramble

Janine contacted me as she was very concerned about her cat Bramble who, it transpired, had growled at her and gone into a deep decline since being shown the dead body of the family's other cat Merlin, who had died. I normally feel this is a good thing, so that animals can understand that their animal friend has passed, as they are normally far more accepting than us humans! However, this seemed to send Bramble into a complete sense of shock and caused her to hide almost constantly upstairs under a bed. Bramble had a problem with her foreleg that seemed to refuse to heal and trying to treat it made her even more agitated and depressed.

This is what Janine had to say:

My name is Janine and I have a cat that I have had since she was a kitten, we have been together 15 years, her name is Bramble, I would like a reading as she has had some health issues recently and I am hoping you may be able to help. I know we have shared a past life, as she once told me. I would really like to know more about how I can help her.

Kind regards Janine

The following reading is what I intuited from Bramble, so that she could help Janine understand why she had been so upset to see Merlin's body and also about the whole family's connections through many lifetimes!

<u>Reading for Janine and Bramble 6/04/12</u>

Dear Janine

Herewith some information from Bramble

Disconnected, Fearful of Life

I feel poor Bramble has just disconnected from the trauma of what happened with Merlin, which indeed triggered a past life where I feel they were both human - which I hope doesn't sound too weird! I feel the swelling in the right foreleg is the last residues working their way out. I feel they were in a battle or fight and that Bramble was always looking out for the person who was Merlin and he would lead the man that was Bramble, into very tricky situations that Bramble would always have to find a way out of. Having said that they do really love each other - they could even have been brothers, which of course can be annoying as Bramble found with Merlin in this lifetime, but of course loved deeply (I know they weren't related in this life-time , but came to be living together so that this could finally be resolved). I think seeing his body (which I agree would normally be a good thing), just triggered so much deep memory of loss that she found it almost unbearable and on some level will have held you responsible, which is why she growled and was so fearful of everything. Of course it wasn't your fault and you were only trying to do what you thought right - which under normal circumstances, would have been. I feel now that you might have been their parents and that you will have done your best, but that your husband - their father, would have encouraged them both to prove themselves on the battlefield and be warriors, which of course you would have hated, but never the less would have done your best to protect them, which is why you always try to be so nurturing in this life! I feel in the battle or fight that the brothers were involved in, Bramble's right arm was badly injured and I feel became infected and maybe caused a withering, which was a constant reminder of the awful sense of loss and guilt, as Merlin as the human brother, had been killed. Any issue with the shoulders are about shouldering responsibility on an emotional level, and as it's the right shoulder and arm it's the masculine side and so will be connected to a male energy - either a deep connection with a human man or a male animal, and seeing as so much was triggered by Merlin's passing, this seems right to me that

21

Bramble is trying to work through the last residues of this. I asked the question as to whether you were involved in this past life and she said that both you and your husband were. The whole reason why the cats came to you was to reconnect with each other and you and your husband and work through this trauma that was still locked in and buried in the psyche. I'm sure your husband is a very good person, but how would you say his relationship with animals is? Would you say that rather than being a total enthusiast and loving having a house full of animals, he will have come to it gradually? It would just be very interesting to know his views and reactions to all the animals in your household now!

I feel if we can re-write the past life and heal all the trauma, then Bramble will be able to let her guilt go and start to fully enjoy feeling safe and get her cat life back! It's so interesting about her stiffness, as arthritis is linked with very blocked emotions within us and a possible stubbornness or reluctance to address issues, which I think would make sense as poor Bramble obviously hasn't wanted to revisit the pain of losing Merlin in either lifetime! However the swelling does tell me that things are coming to a head and that on some level she's ready to let it go at last. I feel some homeopathic remedies or flower essences would help, but have a think and have a chat with me about your husband's connection with your lovely pets - I'm NOT suggesting that he's unkind in any shape or form - He would have been doing what he thought was right in that lifetime! But it will be very interesting to have a chat and see if we can finally release all this for Bramble at last.

Janine and I had a great re-write session together; where both sons had survived and gone on to lead less dangerous lives, with fewer risky escapades. Janine also said that her husband hadn't really been an 'animal' person before, but had had to begin to like the cats, as it was a case of 'love me love my cats!' This is what Janine had to say after our session.

I just wanted to thank you again for the reading, and to say that I have been talking to Bramble about what you wrote, and she seems to really be taking notice of me and doing a lot ofpurring. I feel really positive about the future and already feel that my connection with Bramble has improved almost back to how we were before Merlin died. This is amazing in such a short period of time.

I didn't get a chance to tell you that I do healing, mainly with animals, using energy healing and also using crystals, Bramble responds very well to healing, but although her arm is stable, it wasn't getting any better, I realized then that this was beyond my knowledge and she needed more than just healing.

My husband is very fascinated by your reading, luckily for me doing healing, he is very open minded, I did actually joke with him that he had been married to me once before and chose to do it again in this life, he must be a glutton for punishment!

My dog can't be left - I can't get on with my life!

The following fascinating case from a lady in California, which was really intriguing and so interesting to hear what she had to say in reply to Mojo's reading!

Anne was having a terrible time trying to leave her dog Mojo at home, on the occasions that it was not appropriate for him to be with her. Because of the difficulties she felt that she was being limited in getting' out there' and pursuing her career as a therapist and just somehow getting on with her life. She was also experiencing physical pain in the right side of her body that would go into spasms. She was feeling completely blocked and although she adored her dog - things were becoming tense!

Reading for Anne and Mojo 11/04/12

Dear Anne
Herewith some information from Mojo.

Loving Protector

23

There are several layers to this and I'm not at all surprised that his eyes 'called' you, as he had to find his way back to you this time around in order to resolve unfinished business from the past!

The past life trauma that he's trying to help you let go of is one where he feels guilty for not stopping you doing something, or supporting you better, because of the outcome, and you feel fearful on a subconscious level about 'stepping out' because of this past traumatic outcome. I feel that Mojo was your father in this past life and it feels like a lifetime in England. You were one very headstrong girl and decided to leave home to search employment in a man's world. Your father expected you to just marry you so you could breed children - this was not for you! Interesting that Mojo's breed is of British origin (only just thought that!) I can see you in a carriage with four horses galloping along and then something happened to make the carriage tip over and you were thrown to your death. I think you had just run away with some savings - very hard in those days and your father never recovered from his guilt of not listening to your needs and helping you more or protecting you in a way that you could be happy.

So Mojo is still holding that guilt and finds it very difficult when you are out of his sight or not travelling with you (which is most significant) where he can monitor your safety. If he's in the car, he can be sure that he will be overseeing your safety. I'm not in any way suggesting that you are unsafe travelling with or without him - it's  *just the old trauma stuck in there rearing its ugly head for you both! This also impacts on your confidence in going forwards -*

getting yourself out there because of the terrible outcome in the past. Mojo is here to help you release this, because he is limiting you. There are several layers to this and I'm not at all surprised that his eyes 'called' you, as he had to find his way back to you this from doing things you want to do for the very reason that it is flagged up and addressed! There is a deep block inside you that prevents you from going forward and Mojo is just mirroring this by your feeling that he is preventing you from leaving him, and doing what you would like to - interesting that horses also come into the equation as horses and transport were responsible for the tragedy in the past life. Mojo has been so quick to show me these very vivid scenes from the past in great detail, so it's very much to the fore of his mind and he desperately wants to let go of the guilt he's held for so long - I'm getting 1800s? What better way to return to give you that unconditional love that was so denied to you in that past, by coming back as a very strong character dog! His whole presence is strong and he has chosen a very robust kind of breed to be your protector in a canine form! I don't think he seems overtly protective of you - there are just all these undercurrents going on. This is why he needs to be in the car with you, making sure you're safe. Getting another dog at the moment will not alleviate anything; we need to resolve this cellular memory. I will dowse and see what I can suggest as a remedy that can support the work we can do to re-write this. Perhaps you could imagine this life and what you would have looked like.

Imagine what Mojo might have looked like - I'm getting that he had a large whiskery moustache! But see what you get. Imagine perhaps leaving with his blessing and a safe journey in the carriage or perhaps him travelling with you allowing you to take up a career with good grace? Play around with these suggestions and see which resonate with you the most. If you sit with Mojo when you are doing this - he will show you the images in your mind and help you resolve them for both your sakes.

I feel sure this will help him feel more relaxed about you leaving him and you will feel freer to do what you want with confidence and lose your self-doubt. I feel there are some energies around your home that might need some clearing - nothing nasty, maybe some horses and soldiers from a past battle or something like that? Don't know if that makes sense? You can go out wherever you feel drawn and imagine creating a pillar of light up to the heavens and invite anything or anyone, to be lifted up to go to the light. Make sure you wrap yourself in protection first by visualising a colour and then a shape and then imagine sitting inside it wrapped in loving protection e.g. a pink bubble? - Mojo will show you how as he's the expert!

As I said sit with Mojo and visualise the tragedy, knowing you are safe, as though you are just watching a movie and then, as the director of this movie, change the whole outcome to create a happy, safe resolution and then really breathe in that feeling of safety and fulfilment, so that every cell is filled with this new memory, that will allow you both to go forwards without limitation or fear. If you have any difficulty let me know and I can guide you through it!

I do hope this has been of help in understanding why Mojo is like he is and what this has brought up for you.

Very best wishes Madeleine

This was Anne's reply! I think you'll agree it's pretty fascinating!

Hi, Madeleine,

I cannot believe how incredibly accurate you are and how this story mirrors so much of my growing up too!!! We also had English bulldogs!

*My father, in real life, was adamant with me and every time I asked to do something I wanted to do (and it was always something that took me away from him) I always **got a BIG NO!** I was expected to be pretty and get married. **I never wanted to marry,** although I did, (but I am and I have been interested in the spiritual side of energy for years and years.*

26

This is the story I have been looking for, for so long!
All my later boyfriends had moustaches and were very
controlling! I know that this does not exactly make sense,
maybe, in connection with Mojo, but it is so incredibly uncanny
the similarities. My father was Australian and had an English
type accent, very handsome and dark, even though I am very
light.

Also I have a love of horses, AND I also have a 'fear' that has
never made sense to anyone. This is a fear that can freeze me
and stop me in my tracks, especially when I am on the ground
and they start to act up. I jump out of the way and everyone
gets annoyed, but I can't help it. I always felt that this fear was
tied in to being trampled by carriage horses in England in the
1800', but I never was able to shift it!!

This all makes so much sense and resonates within me deeply; I
feel that I can now re-write the story as now I have the whole
picture; it feels like the pieces to the puzzle finally fell into
place!!

Thank YOU, Anne.

I think you'll agree that Mojo's message to me was pretty
accurate! I was so pleased that Anne now understood why
Mojo behaved the way that he did, and that they could
understand each other far better. Very often just by airing
these kinds of issues and animals realise that we finally
'get it'; they can relax and know that their work is done
and everyone can get on with their lives!

More grieving for sons

I received a message from a lady called Sabine from
Switzerland, who was still suffering terrible grief at the
passing of her dog Kismet. As you will see they had an
extraordinary connection, which was trying to surface
when they were together as human and dog, but in order
to understand the intensity of the grief, we had to delve a
little deeper to make sense of it.

These were Sabine's questions to ask Kismet in spirit;

What soul connection do we have?
Is he still communicating with me?

Why was I unable to spend all my time with him and always needed a commercial dog sitter which hurt me deeply. When Kismet died I was visiting relatives in Germany and had no chance to pat him and say goodbye personally. I did my best all the time with him and he gave me so much love eternally, he felt like my baby son. Sometimes I was talking to him in some ancient language of the South Seas; I had no idea though what it was about! Will I see him again?

Reading for Sabine and Kismet 14/05/13

Dear Sabine,

Herewith some information from dear Kismet.

Eternal soul connection

*Wow I've rarely come across two more deeply entwined souls before you two! I always ask for a word or phrase that underpins the reading and this is what I get for Kismet. There are **soul mates** and there are soul mates. It feels like you two have been around each other's energy forever. In fact it doesn't seem to feel complete in each incarnation unless you reconnect at least once or twice each time, either as humans or animals. I think you've both tried out various physical bodies to see how you can best serve each other on your combined and individual Soul journeys.*

It feels right for the moment that he is in spirit as pure energy, as he seems to be telling me that it's time for lots of wisdom you've been acquiring or 'remembering', that needs to be assimilated at this time. You've been on quite a journey together experiencing and surviving all kinds of challenges.

I feel that although it was very sad that you weren't able to say goodbye to him properly, on a 3 dimensional level I think he wanted to save you the trauma of seeing him pass, but also to

28

make you address your perceptions and issues around the emotion of guilt. He says you are very good at beating yourself up and diminishing your power through this, which only leads to, and feeds, your sense of unworthiness? He knows you absolutely did your best for him, but he says you are a very driven person, always feeling that you have to prove yourself to others, but more importantly to yourself and whatever you do, you never think that it's good enough? Sometimes you self-sabotage by a fear of failing and then when it does go wrong, you just blame yourself and your perceived inadequacies. Kismet says this is all in your head and that you are such an honourable person. If only you would believe it!

As to your feelings about not spending as much time with him as you would have wished - this is a very 3 dimensional concept. Because you are so connected it didn't matter really where you were in the world, you were always right next to each other - as I said it's still hard to distinguish where one ends and the other starts, you're so completely connected - this continues to apply, even though Kismet is not actually in a physical body at this time. So he is totally around you guiding and supporting you, like a silent partner!

There are many layers to your past lives and I'm very interested in the South Seas influence, and how those lifetimes created some of your self-doubt and self-blame. I'm seeing a Polynesian lifetime, where you were a tribe of great seafarers. When I look at your photo I start to see lots of tattoos on your face and your eyes darkening, with strange plaits and designs in your hair - you are male and I feel that Kismet was your son in this life. He's showing me that you seemed to always be looking for the next adventure, or new land to conquer. You were very proud and against advice, set off on a journey with your son, in a beautiful reed boat.

Unfortunately the storm that had been predicted blew up and capsized the boat. The seas were huge and you all perished. Seeing your son die was so awful and your dying thoughts were that you had been so foolish and were heartbroken that you had caused your son's death. I'm also getting a lifetime where you inhabited Easter Island and that you worked on the incredible figures there. Of course the people there didn't fare very well as they ran out of wood and food and many perished - creating more self-blame? - I don't know if this has been a place that has interested you?

I can also see you in a beautiful feather cloak with a large wooden club, as an early Maori settler - you seem to have had many lifetimes as a man. Kismet seems to have tried various physical vehicles, but sometimes he was just a guide, overseeing your progress. I feel the reason that he passed without your physical presence this time, is that he knew how distraught you were when you watched him drown in that past life and he wanted to spare you that experience this time around. I feel that it would be useful to imagine different outcomes between you, where perhaps you sail to safety and find an abundant, safe island to inhabit. You can see if you get any images and then make sure that you change the whole feel of the end result - always change the ending to one of safety and love. I feel this is definitely why Kismet chose to come back as a dog this time around, as it was the best way to shower you in unconditional love! It was also the best way to get inside your heart, as human relationships can be far harder to trust to let in!

I feel he will come back as a dog again, once you have healed this issue from the past so that you can have a very happy, blame free future life together. He has given you such a gift of the opportunity to heal this once and for all, so that you can feel so much better about yourself. Your soul contracts committed to this ending, in order to bring all this up to be finally healed, released and forgiven.

Let me know how this resonates with you and if you visualised any images or felt emotions come up whilst reading these words from Kismet.

This is the perfect time to be free! If you did visualise any images, let me know how you might have created a far happier outcome - so creating a whole new dimension where the old trauma never happened and so you only store or bring back the happy memories. This paves the way for creating more happy times together, not only with Kismet but also yourself. Remember that we can create our realities by healing the past and with these techniques, we can certainly even change the past - relinquishing it's emotional and physical hold on us!

This was Sabine's reply!

Dear Madeleine

When reading your wonderful lines again and being touched ever so much by your dear words about Kismet and me - I heard the following ancient words like a little song I would sing within my heart for Kismet:

> *"Ne le moku, taki, me te poku e ta pe,*
> *mukataliq n li kopo takin,*
> *mathsu, ruhi te po, maki ro ro"*

MATALA

I received this translation for the song from within:

"My little child, I am so sad losing you. The eternal flame in our hearts will be shining bright forever. I promise you that we will always be sharing eternal love together"

I love you
MATALA (mother)

I feel that Kismet and I lived on Roratonga island 1261 - 1299 in the Southern Pacific - and with our beautiful reed boat we had gone towards Tongatapu - of which we had heard that it was a gateway island or stepping stone to a cascade of islands eventually leading to "Uossa" which was our word for Australia.

When I applied a healing ending, it evolved in a way that we had gone around the island for around two days being greeted by different people, who invited us to their village to rest and eat with them, exchanging stories almost like a modern telephone service and a wise medicine man had decided to go with us on

'Some angels chose fur instead of wings'

our reed boat to cross the strait of around 50 km between the islands. When the storm started moving in, we had only just been out one hour from the island and decided to turn our boat and head back; but the heavy winds caused us to be adrift and so we were washed up a long distance further on a small island with huge coconut trees and many tortoises who adored this small paradisiacal island which had only a very small tribe living on it, but their hospitality was very great and we stayed with them and learned a lot about fishing from the ocean and what leaves to eat from shrubs, which would contain vitamins, but our main food was fish and coconut milk and we had a very fulfilled life on that island together, enjoying nature so much and the company of our new found clan or family. Kismet was very much loved by everyone and I had such a respect and love of his wisdom which seemed to pour from his little child heart - an energy that has come out so much again in this life with him here in Switzerland - it was always about the heart that really matters and is the strongest bond.

I look forward to hearing of Kismet's return to continue their love in the physical realms once more!

Chapter 3

A Safe Place to Conceive

The following case studies show where animals have led their owners back to past lives, where there has been trauma connected to their pregnancies and situations where it has been very unsafe to have a child. These traumas are stored at a cellular level, and can prevent people conceiving and having the child that they've always dreamed of in their current life. When the animals take you back to those times, you can heal and release those memories. This chapter shows how miracles can happen when you can change your DNA memory - thanks to the wisdom of your pets and sometimes slightly larger animals!

Bethany and Cosmos create a miracle

I received an email from Bethany who lives in Namibia, who had a very distressing story.

Hi, I live in Otjiwarongo in Namibia. I have just bought your book the Whale Whisperer, and found it a very emotional read. Whales have always fascinated me and I have been told that I have a whale connection. I feel I am in a very bad emotional state right now. I have had six miscarriages, the last one due to a negative entity which touched me in the night. The fear of not being able to have a child is keeping me from moving forward.

I also have a horse named Cosmos. I know he is in my life to help me, but don't know if I am always listening correctly, am I putting too much of my fears on to him?

I also try to give him as much freedom as I can. It would be great to hear from you.

Reading for Bethany and Cosmos 14/03/12

Dear Bethany

Herewith some information for you,

I am so sorry you've had such a dreadful time. There are several layers to this. Mainly the thing that seems to be preventing you carrying full term is a subconscious fear that your baby will not be safe in the world. This stems from at least two past lives, which I will describe now and apologise if it sounds too way out or distressing for you, but we do need to access this and then we can just change the whole past outcomes!! But I know you said you have a deep connection to whales. I can see that you have been a southern right whale - interesting as I met them at Hermanus bay in South Africa. They migrate immense distances with their young and are tormented by orca who hunt their offspring.

I feel that this happened on more than one occasion! Also there is a past Roman life, obviously as a human. There was a lot of jealousy around and it felt like you were very high up even perhaps an emperor's wife or consort. I feel you were killed whilst you were pregnant, or certainly made to abort your baby. However distressing as I absolutely know it has been to lose your babies, it will have been the soul fragments trying to experience being with you again and in some way help you get to the point where you can release the fear and know without doubt that it can be safe for you to deliver a healthy baby. I feel that the negative entity could have been created or attracted from your subconscious fear. This is nothing to blame yourself for! It is totally understandable that you would have these fears. We just need to get you to forgive yourself and release that entire past trauma. We can do this by skype in a re-write session where we change the whole outcome. Cosmos is trying to support you so much and is such a grounding energy - a very special horse and totally meant to be with you at this moment in time - I feel you have lived several lifetimes together when he has tried to protect you, and maybe failed at times - he certainly doesn't want to do that again!

This was Bethany's reply

34

"This was not too weird, some things definitely make more sense to me now, of course there is still so much more I want to know/ find out. I have always been fascinated by soul connections and just did not find the right material to help me."

Bethany and I had a wonderful re-write session where we visualised the rest of her whale pod protecting her and her calf against the orca. She then visualised a timeline over several years where she saw her future calves maturing and becoming grown members of the pod. This felt wonderful and gave her such a feeling of safety, support and protection. We also rewrote the Roman trauma by seeing a wonderful man, that we felt was Cosmos, hiding her away and helping her escape any persecution, allowing her to deliver her baby son and live a simple, happy life away from all the intrigue and debauchery of the Roman court. Again Bethany felt such a feeling of contentment and peace.

We also performed a pre-birth soul contract renewal, where she chose to have a safe and happy life with children from now on. I intuited two beings waiting in the wings to come in as her children, which made me feel very hopeful for her to now feel safe to conceive and carry her baby full term, having the life that she'd always wanted as a mother, watching her child grow up in love and safety.

I was so thrilled to receive this message from Bethany!

22/01/2013

I just wanted to let you know I am 15 weeks pregnant, so far everything ok. It has been a bit of a rollercoaster ride, I get panic attacks that something can go wrong again, but otherwise it is going ok. I know in my heart everything will be ok, but my head goes off on its own.

Love Bethany

We had a 'top up' session together to help allay Bethany's

natural feelings of anxiety, which really seemed to calm her. Cosmos has a new friend of a lovely grey mare to keep him company when Bethany is rather occupied with her new baby. The last I heard from Bethany she was due to have her baby any minute and had a wonderful trouble free pregnancy. I look forward to hearing her news of her baby's safe delivery!

News Flash from Bethany!

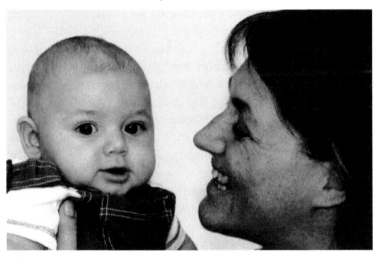

Hi, just wanted to let u know that on Sunday 14th my little boy was born at 18h25. We are doing very well and at home already. He is a very strong little boy, lifts his head up already and keeps it there. He is so adorable and I am so happy that he is at last here!! I will send you pictures via email today. Both of us can't thank you enough for what you have done to get us together!! Lots of love and hugs from the two of us.

Extra update since concluding the book over time - Bethany has also safely given birth to a new daughter, so completing her family - I feel that the two lovely souls waiting in the wings from her soul contract meeting, have now finally found their way back into the physical, where they can reunite with their mother in a safe and beautiful loving environment - what a great ending to such a formerly sad story!

When I was working in France, I was called out to see a lovely lady called Diane, who was concerned about her cat CC. She wondered whether she would cope with their imminent house move, as CC was blind and managed fairly well in her familiar surroundings, but Diane really wasn't sure she'd be ok in a new home.

Diane was expecting her first child, but had had to rearrange our appointment, due to an emergency visit to the doctors. She explained that she's had three miscarriages and was naturally very concerned about the progress of her baby when she started to bleed. Diane rested on the sofa with her cats all around her, especially CC who sat on the arm of the chair looking very lethargic and a little sad. She was extremely overweight, but Diane said that she's always been that way and she had tried everything to keep her weight down and that she really didn't eat that much. She also said that CC had been blind ever since she'd rescued her several years ago, as no-one else would re-home her. Diane wanted to know what their connections were, as she'd felt compelled to give her a home as though she had no choice in the matter - which of course we shall see - Diane hadn't! As CC slept on the sofa, she hadn't opened her eyes at all, but although she seemed to be in deep slumber, she started to 'talk' to me about Diane's pregnancy and her fears concerning carrying her baby to full term. This recurring theme of anxiety around safety arose once more.

CC began to transmit some very curious images into my mind, where I saw a very thin aged lion with cloudy eyes as though he was going blind. I felt this was a symptom of something to do with a tsetse fly bite. The old lion, who I felt was CC, was rapidly losing his strength and ability to protect the pride from marauding younger males, who wanted to assume leadership of the pride, which would mean the old lion being killed or very badly wounded and left to die an agonising death as his pride was taken from him. CC told me that Diane was one of his lionesses with cubs and that a new male had come and had a terrible fight with the old lion who mortally wounded, starved and died. Tragically when a new male takes over a pride, he kills all of the old male's offspring, so that the lionesses come into season and can breed with him and produce his cubs. All of Diane's cubs were killed.

CC felt so devastated at not being able to protect his pride and that he'd failed in his duty to them. Being so thin had made CC over compensate in her present incarnation to always carry enough weight in case of lean times. Diane had that residual fear of it being an unsafe world to bring her young into the world, like Bethany. So with CC's help, we created a whole new scenario, where everyone could be safe, fulfilled and happy. I was fascinated to hear when I recounted CC's visions that Diane had previously lived in South Africa, before relocating to France, so she was able to visualise the lion scenes very clearly! Diane visualised the cubs growing bigger and stronger and the lionesses managing to make kills to support and feed the old lion, who finally died of old age and natural causes.

Some of the male cubs left, but two brothers took over the pride and the female cubs remained to be part of the hunting team of the pride. Diane saw her cubs mature and live strong, wild lives and I asked her to really feel into her sense of satisfaction of expanding the strength of the pride where it could flourish. This seemed to give her an enormous sense of satisfaction of working with nature and playing such an important role in creating new life to fulfil her role as a mother.

A great sense of peace seemed to permeate from them both. When we'd completed the re-write CC suddenly opened her eyes and they were milky white just like the lion's eyes that she'd shown me! I hope that I will receive good news from Diane about the safe delivery of her baby soon!

More traumas around pregnancy and conception …

Here is an email I received from a devastated Tina, desperate to find some answers to the seemingly meaningless death of her lovely cat Reggie…

Tina and Reggie

Hi Madeline,

Since the death of my precious little kitty Reggie, I have tried to seek solace and make sense of his death and began reading your book.

Four chapters in and I'm now itching to know more about the past life of my kitty, and if there's any way of knowing if we will be re-united.

I still cry myself to sleep at night, he was my baby, and he celebrated his first birthday on the 15th of February and was hit by a car two days later on the 17th.

I was on a business trip when it happened and have not forgiven myself for leaving, despite leaving my family in charge, I still feel responsible for his death.

Nobody looked after him and worried like I did. We were only together for 10 months, he came into my life on the 8th of April, I was never a cat person, but the first time I laid eyes on him, I was besotted by him and he changed my life. If you have any way of communicating with him, please let him know I'm sorry I wasn't there to protect him that night, and I love and miss him very much.

This is what I intuited from Reggie.

Dear Tina

Herewith some information from Reggie

Loving Soul Reconnection / love, love, love!

I always ask for a word or phrase that might underpin the reading and this is what I get from Reggie.

This is a real soul mate connection, which is why you feel so devastated without his physical presence. At this moment in time there must seem like there is no sense to why he had such a short life when he was SO loved and cherished!

Understanding our soul journeys can feel so hard and indeed harsh when sometimes loved ones only choose to incarnate for a very short time, just to reconnect with us and perhaps help to release past life traumas - or raise awareness as to why these heart breaks devastate us so much!

This beautiful loving being, chose to reconnect with you just for a short time to feel your presence once more and to help you begin to comprehend the concept of eternal life - I absolutely know that's very little consolation at the moment, but in time you will begin to understand, just right now that's a bit of a step too far!

If you've read my book "Your Pets' Past Life" You will have read about my lovely Kittie Thebes who was also killed by a car, when he was 8 months old. I couldn't believe that he would come with SO much love and then leave me so soon! I was completely heart broken. He was the most incredible healer and regularly assisted me with my human clients by giving amazing healing and information about their traumas, even from when he was a tiny bundle of fluff!

So I know exactly what you are going through. I feel that Reggie was the 'glue' that kept you together - I get the feeling and the image of you almost blending into one, as though he would snuggle in so close, as though he would have climbed inside your skin if he could have! He was a part of you - almost the best part of you, is what you thought, so without his physical presence you feel so lost.

Being away when it happened I know makes it even harder to bear and I know how much you blame yourself. We have to keep reminding ourselves of the bigger picture. I feel he chose to leave whilst you were away, because he knew he had to and if you were there, he would have found it so difficult, as he loved (and loves you) so much!

What I saw when I asked Thebes WHY??? He told me that when he was born, he still was connected to his spirit body by a silver cord that didn't break and that he was contracted to visit just for this short time and I'm getting the same image from Reggie. Thebes told me that he left because he felt he could help me far more from spirit and that there was a lot of work that I had to do and if he'd stayed, I would never have wanted to leave him and that I MUST do this work now!

Again I feel this is what Reggie is saying to you! There are things you must take forwards in your life - important things that have much bigger consequences and benefits than even you can comprehend right now. He WILL come back to you because he has to - there is no separation, but for now you have to take all the opportunities coming your way. I'm not sure what your current work is, but Reggie is saying that there is much more to do with healing both for people and the planet coming your way and all this sadness is preparing you for your future work in helping others understand more about the grand plan that spirit has organised for us.

Reggie is right behind you guiding you forwards - when I had to speak at a very big scary conference in New Zealand, I saw and felt Thebes walk up my bed in the hotel room and then proceeded to 'tell' me exactly what to say in my presentation! I was so ecstatic that he had come from spirit to guide me, but of course that is what he said he would do!

I feel him very strongly now as I'm writing this - he is very keen to explain what Reggie's soul purpose is for you!

Reggie is showing me a former lifetime, where he was your beloved child. Tragically you died very soon after giving birth with him cradled in your arms. He was a little boy and had to somehow cope with growing up without you. However, he always felt your guiding presence through the many challenges that he faced and you would draw close to him from spirit! I don't know whether you have had any issues with fertility (sorry if this is a bit personal) but Reggie is trying to explain why you may have had some issues or fears about this?? I don't know if this makes sense, but he seems very keen to share this with you. Let me know if this might be so, as we could work to heal this if necessary. This is why you recognised him the first time you saw him and there was no way that you couldn't be together. You just felt that profound connection and that was it! He made you remember that you are worthy of being loved - that you are worthy. So please don't blame yourself. In that past life you gave him life, you guided his life, as he grew into a wonderful young man.

I think this is why you always worried about him so much, as on some level you still remembered the physical separation, but also the concern of watching over him when he might have made mistakes.

So I feel once your life challenges have been understood and you have found your path, which Reggie will always be guiding you on, he will come back to you. I feel he will be another cat, as he loved the feeling of his feline body and also he says that it is a wonderful way to get close to you! So have faith he will always be with you on a soul level - this is one of the hardest things for us to accept. Death seems to be so final, but the animals have told me so often that it's just like being in another room eavesdropping!

He says that he still comes to you at night in your bed and he says watch out for a sudden feeling of heat - like a warm surge - allow him to comfort you in this way, also sit in one of his favourite spots in the house and send a cord of love from your heart to his. This might be a bit emotional, but he will connect with you and let you know that he's around.

He's showing me a beautiful silver tabby with some white patches - lovely white paws. So this might be his future incarnation. He will find you in an unexpected way so just be open -

you don't need to go searching as he will find YOU when the time is right - not quite yet, but have no fear he is always near!

This was Tina's reply

Hi Madeline,

Thank you..

I had a feeling that he was my son, maybe we should do a session on conception, children, pregnancy etc...

Since Reggie left, I have had this strong sense of - I'm ready to love and nurture, I feel so empty and my life feels so pointless without having a little somebody to come home to love and look after. I feel like my time to start a family is drawing closer. But despite wanting to have a family, I'm also petrified of the actual birthing process. It has always mortified me to the point where I never really thought I would ever want children because of the pain involved. (I'm starting to understand why!)

I also worry about the financials of having a baby, I feel like I need to be prepared to have to raise him/her on my own, (not sure why I've always felt that way even though I have a husband) and despite my best efforts to have my business successfully up and running, I keep facing obstacles to the point where I lately began to question if I'm even supposed to be in this trade or will I be doing something else. I hope he can guide me. Another fear was/is if my husband and I conceive now, would I bring his soul back and lose him again very quickly if he hadn't learnt all his karmic lessons, but I think you've put my mind at ease that he will come back as a kitty again. (I'm not sure if you picked up on a termination, but that also happened at 17 - I've kept that from everybody in my life, and if there's anything that needs to be "cleared' from it, I guess now might be the right time)

Tina and I had a lovely session together after the reading to re-write her past life with Reggie. We visualised her survival of the birth - in fact we saw it being a really quick and easy birth of her beautiful son. Both went on to have happy, healthy lives, always supporting each other, even through a role reversal, when Tina became old and could no longer look after herself. Reggie as her son always looked after her until she passed. By changing the whole outcome and creating a new dimension where the trauma never happened, Tina can choose to only allow the cell memories from that new story to impact on her. This can allow her DNA to be reprogrammed into knowing that bringing a child into this world can be a safe and wonderful experience.

By releasing the fear, everything can change!

Chapter 4

Overcome Your Self-Limiting Fear and Pain, with a Little Help from Your Animal Friends

Reading for Mary and Cleo

Dear Mary

Herewith some information from Cleo

Teacher/soul companion/soul star family connection

I always ask for a word or phrase that might underpin the reading and this is what I get from Cleo.

I can see why you were so devastated at her passing at such a young age - you must have felt very cheated at only being together for such a short time. It's also so tragic that she was so poorly at the end of her life, not having the long, happy, care free life that she should have. That's the human perspective, which of course is completely natural and why we are here - to experience these very challenging emotions of which grief and guilt are the hardest to understand and work through.

As you so rightly feel, this was no ordinary connection between you (not that any connection is really ordinary!) But this connection between the two of you is so profound and eternal. Cleo came for only a brief time to experience being with you once again in different forms and to remind your soul of the never ending love between you. I keep seeing Cleo, as a magical white wolf cub with you as her mother. I feel Carrie and some of your other dogs were also members of the same pack. Cleo is showing me this lifetime where there were some cruel trappers who set traps and wanted to steal Cleo, so that they could raise her and eventually kill her for her pelt. Tragically you got trapped by your left paw in one of these awful traps and were unable to return to the den to protect Cleo. Carrie was a young wolf from another litter, who tried to look after Cleo, but she was scared away by the trappers, who managed to grab Cleo and steal her away. Meanwhile you were desperately trying to escape from the trap and in the end had to chew your paw to free yourself. When you got back to the den, it was too late - Cleo had been stolen. You felt such sadness at not being able to be there to protect her and your remaining paw got infected and I think that the combination of the grief and the infection eventually caused your death. Cleo was never really fed the right food and so her fragile digestion suffered and she also succumbed to trauma and malnutrition.

I don't know whether she had digestive organ problems when she was with you in this lifetime? I feel that the pain in your fingers and any health issues that Cleo experienced are all tied in with this past life!

So perhaps you could visualise being back there, but this time create a much happier safer outcome? Create a whole new story, where you were both safe and that the whole pack had a long, happy, wild existence. Perhaps you could re-script the whole story, where you had been aware of the trappers' intentions and so moved the whole pack higher up in the mountains (I'm being told Montana?), where the trappers couldn't find you and then you could live out the long, safe, happy, wild life together. Maybe if you can visualise this - see your left forepaw looking strong, whole and healthy - really embrace the whole feeling of unity and safety between you, Cleo, Carrie and all the other wolf family. I think this re-write would really help lessen the need for your body to create pain in your left hand fingers, because of the perpetuated cell memories of trauma still stored there. If the memory is healed then so can the need to feel the physical pain there! There may also be some essences you could take to help relieve this. The Orchid essence "Releasing Karmic Patterns" and "Karmic Calm", might well be of help, also the Australian Bush Flower essence "Boab", which helps in healing ancestral past life traumas. You can have a look at these essences on www.healingorchids.com to see what you think? Maybe every time you might feel pain in your

hand, visualise your lovely strong healthy wolf paw!! I feel that when Cleo passed, the other pack members were there in spirit waiting for her giving her healing. I also see a mother energy person who had loved dogs on the earthly realm - or someone who would have been a great mentor for you with your passion for dogs - it feels like someone who would have taken you under their wing - it maybe your mother or grandmother, but someone who treated you this way??

I don't feel that Cleo has come back yet in this current life - I feel she may have sent you other animals for whatever reason that they needed to be with you.

Cleo has taught you so much and is continuing to do so, in that she is helping you understand the eternal flame I think the 'distancing' herself near the end, was just her way of having some 'time out' to process everything she needed to before she left, so try not to feel too sad about this or blame yourself. She says that she went when the time was right, so don't beat yourself up any more about it! I also see her as this white wolf star being with a big connection to Sirius where you also shared *lifetimes as star beings.   So you have experienced so many incarnations in many different forms on your soul journey together and you will experience many more.   I feel at the moment that she finds being in spirit as a pure energy form, much easier, as she was so sensitive to the heavy energies of three dimensional earth - now the earth's vibration is changing so dramatically, she will be able to return and cope much better, especially if this traumatic life that she flagged up can be healed. If you have any difficulty with this let me know and we could have a skype or phone call to go through it together, but see how you get on!*

I do hope this helps you understand your incredible, profound connection, with this beautiful dog.

Much love
Madeleine

Mary's reply

Dear Madeleine,

Thank you so much for your communication with darling Cleo. It brought me such joy and peace and for that I am so grateful. I would like if I may, to just tell you about a few things that Cleo said that are so relevant to me.

When I was 12 years old I asked my father if I could have a German Shepherd dog. His reply was "I am not having a wolf in the house! I replied "Well that is why I want one because I love wolves." (It wasn't until I was in my late 20's that I had my first GSD.) I have always loved wolves ever since I can remember. I have in my home, pictures of wolves, along with two wolf calendars that I renew every year. My spirit guide is a wolf. I feel so very close to them and I also buy any books on wolves. Cleo's illness was epilepsy and she had her first fit aged 14 months. After her death I researched epilepsy in GSD'S and Dr Malcolm Wallis told me that Cleo's grandfather 7 generations back had been an epileptic. She was the only one of her litter that was an epileptic, because I checked about her brothers and sisters. Needless to say I never bred a litter of puppies again and that was my first litter. In 2001 I visited a friend in Denmark and she had booked us in with a clairvoyant for a reading. It was a present from my friend to me. In my reading with him he said this " You have a lot of moments in your life when you feel (quite rightly) that you don't belong on this planet and that is because you have a very strong connection with Sirius the Dog Planet!" "You have lived there in a previous life". "The connection is so strong that is why you feel so out of place on the Earth Plane".

I will definitely research your very kind suggestion on flower essences.

I have started with great enthusiasm to visualise being back in the wolf story and have made good steps in making the story so different. "It was four in the morning when I sensed danger that the trappers were not far away. I woke the pack up (17 of us) and we hurriedly left and started to move away. We crossed a shallow part in the river and started to climb upwards. We travelled at a trot for many hours and then we rested so the young cubs could sleep. After resting we travelled on and found a "kill" that had been left and so every wolf could feed. There was a lone male wolf near the kill and for the next few days he followed us keeping his distance. Eventually we accepted him into the pack and so we became a pack of 18. He will bring in new bloodlines when the time comes. We are now 150 miles away from our original home, up in the mountains but with a valley near so we can hunt. I tell Cleo repeatedly that we are now safe because no man can follow us where we are as the terrain is too difficult and the winter snows are coming. I feel so safe now and it is so wonderful to have Cleo, Khanna and my other dogs (all in the spirit world now) as members of my wolf pack".

I think it's wonderful and exciting that at some time in the future Cleo will come back to me and you are so so right in saying that I am in an "emotional transience" at the moment. I am not quite sure what I should be doing or how to find that out, also I am not in the right environment physically, I am *such a country person, having lived all my life in the country, but am not living in the country at present, although I am not far from it.*

I just wanted to say that since I have received your communication with Cleo, and re-wrote the wolf story, my fingers have hurt ONLY ONCE and for a very brief time!!

So I am continuing talking to darling Cleo and the pack to reaffirm the new story! This is just wonderful after all these years of pain.

Thank you so much for the reading Madeleine I have just ordered "An Exchange of Love" to read now!

Much love Mary

Reading for Fay and Max 17/03/16

Dear Fay

Herewith some information from dearest Max

Wise Guardian/ Family Soul Mate

I always ask for a word or phrase that might underpin the reading and this is what I get from Max.

Having Max in your life made your home seem like home - there was a sense of completeness having him in your life - which is why it feels so devastating without him!

Of course being a cat they do have an air of independence, but I get the feeling from him that he was always just there. When you came home from a challenging day or situation, things just always felt better when Max appeared! It just felt as though when Max came for a scratch under the chin and gazed at you with his lovely eyes, everything would be ok. Stroking him would somehow ease and drain all your tension and the world would seem a better place, which is why it's so hard not having him with you in the physical!

I feel that Max would filter a lot of stress in the household - not that this is anything to blame yourself for, it was part of his soul contract with you. I get that there were problems with his kidneys and some sort of obstruction in his digestive tract? Did he have any blood tests? As I'm also getting some issues with his liver, shown in his test??

I feel he kept going for as long as he could, but that he let you know when he needed help to transition. He says that he was uncomfortable but that you did exactly the right thing at the right time - even though it was incredibly hard to make that decision to do so! He says there is nothing to forgive - it was the final gift of love that you could give him and if he had lived longer he would have suffered much more.

He's talking about some digestive issues with you or someone close to you in the family?? Something like IBS. He says that this person feels everything in their gut and it's the first place to feel unsettled if there is stress either in work or in the home, for whatever reason. Life can be very stressful for all of us!! My stomach feels really tight and knotted as I'm typing this? He's saying pay attention to diet as there are foods that are eaten that also trigger or exacerbate this?

He says he's around you so much - he's showing me a kind of shadow in a shaft of light, as though you might imagine him out of the corner of you eye. His spirit presence is so tangible, some-times almost as though he might shed some hair or leave a paw print on a windowsill or the floor!

Did you give him prawns or some fishy treat? I keep getting the picture and smell of them! He absolutely knew how much he was and is loved and this is why you were so courageous and unselfish in letting him go when you did!

He keeps showing me a black dog in spirit, who was waiting for Max when he passed, this dog is also part of your soul family, maybe from your childhood, but they seem very good friends? I keep seeing this dog running around wagging his tail. I keep being drawn to his heart centre, where it looks like a patch of white, but it might just be symbolic of the heart to heart connection between you all?

He's showing me a lovely past life, where he was a lynx and I can see you on a homestead as a young teenage girl, who cared for this lynx kitten when his mother was killed and your father brought it home for you to care for. The kitten was so frightened - Its mother had hidden it and was tragically mortally wounded on a hunt and never managed to get back to the baby - I feel that its siblings also died, but this one managed to survive!

With your loving care, it grew strong and very tame and eventually was allowed to return to the wild, where you would often find each other in a loving reconnection. However one day you realised that you had to let him go, as he had found a mate and was becoming truly wild again as he should be. You were very sad in one way, but happy in another that you had managed to give him the life he was meant to have, but that you were also brave enough to set him free.

Max is saying there are parallels in this life, where that was a kind of feeling of saving each other this time around and that ultimately you set him free again. He loved his life with you and I feel sure he will come back to you when the time is right. Ironically he's showing me another cat that looks very lynx like, with spots and very pointed ears - so be open to this cat finding you! Max is receiving a lot of healing in spirit right now, but will oversee your current life experiences for a while, as you work through this stage in your life and understand the concept of eternal soul connections even more. There was a sense of you taking up the reins of your life after your time together in that past life and I get a similar feeling now - there are things you need to accomplish and fulfil your dreams that seem to have been put on hold right now?

Know that Max is right behind you, pushing you forward and will always be with you in one form or another! He really wants you to know this!

I do hope this helps and makes sense! The homeopathic remedy Ignatia 1M can really help with acute grief, so it may help you to come to terms with his passing and allow you to cope a little better.

Much love, Madeleine

Fay's reply

Hello Madeleine

Thank you again, so much.

I have spoken to my mum and she had a black spaniel! Before I was born but when my biggest sister was a baby perhaps it's him?

My other thought might it be my boyfriend's father in animal form? He had very curly almost wiry hair from what I have seen in photos.

Max was very much my boyfriend's cat and I know he silently grieves for his father rather than openly, I wondered if this was some spiritual connection somehow?

I thought you may like to know, when we got Max, my boyfriend was going through a very hard time with work and things were incredibly stressful, he said Max came just when he needed him, that he felt Max was his little office buddy, helping him get through tough times he definitely helped us with his dearness through a very stressful period.

My boyfriend works from home now and Max was always in his office with him on the sofa or under his desk, he said he felt Max knew things were getting better, so Max felt it was ok to leave us, but my boyfriend had so hoped Max would have seen him succeed and that he would have hung on a little longer. He did have kidney problems and various other ailments. I also do suffer from IBS and problems with my tummy.

You mention his white heart centre, Max had a little white patch on his flank in the middle of all his tabby markings, we would always touch it and say that was where God went "poom" sounds silly but... I have sort of put all my creative little projects on hold as well. I must resume them, for Max.

I am intrigued about the lynx and the homestead. I will be watching out for a lynx like cat and yes I do keep seeing him out of the corner of my eye.

Really thank you so very much Madeleine

The next case involves several animals belonging to Anabell, who had had a couple of serious cancer scares and had suffered some very abusive relationships.

Her daughter Clara was also part of this deep soul family connection. This is what her animals had to say and how their combined stories played out to such an incredible resolution. Anabell had mentioned a dog called Alf, her family had owned when she was a young girl and I felt him come through from spirit to guide me to help Anabell the best way I could. His passing had been very traumatic and Anabell had always blamed herself for not being there for him, as she had to be away studying and she had always felt that she had failed him somehow. Anabell asked me to connect to Christo and Balu - gorgeous dogs and her horses Capri, Raven, Latin Love and Camelot.

Readings for Anabell 18/04/16

Dear Anabell

Herewith some information from your beautiful animals.

You have all been on such an amazing journey together, all of you interconnecting and entwining your soul paths, as you of course know already you are one big soul family, including Clara and her horses!

Whilst re-reading your first email, I felt a very strong message from Alf, as though this was a major trigger in creating/ activating, cancer cells in your body. When you got Alf you were just starting in puberty, becoming a young woman and all that entailed. Not being able to say goodbye to him properly, had a very profound and lasting effect on you. You were obviously very connected, as he loved to follow you so much.

I feel that grief and the shock of sudden loss is a major factor and contributor to your unresolved hurts that have manifested within your body.

This might sound very strange, but I keep being shown a

beautiful herd of wild buffalo, with a great white bull, who was the sacred master of the herd and much revered by the indigenous peoples. I feel your husbands were white men who decimated the herd, with no comprehension of the trauma and devastation this caused. I feel in this lifetime, all your animals were together with you as buffalo!

I'm being shown Raven as the incredible white bull and Alf was your buffalo mother - Hannibal was also there! (He dropped in for just a short time to be part of this current incarnation soul healing journey). The men who were your husbands, shot so many of your herd. I keep being shown a tragic image of you as a calf standing next to the bodies and calling out in terror and shock - it's a really distressing image and very upsetting to feel into! This is something we can work on together to re-write, in order to heal it when we have a session - don't worry I'll guide you through the whole process and make it as safe and loving as possible - it will just be like watching a very unpleasant film, but this time we can change the ending!!

All of your animals (including Camelot and Latin Love) and ironically the husbands have all found their way back into your current life, in order to find a way to heal this terrible travesty. Each one has found their way into your heart in order for somehow things to be released or forgiven. Unfortunately regarding your husbands, neither of you were really ready to be healed or forgiven - but this is part of their soul journeys and we can ask their higher selves permission to heal this finally. This is the first time that all of you have reincarnated together, in order to find a way through this.

You are all contractually bound to reconnect in this life to make sense of the shared trauma!

As you probably know cancer is all about unresolved hurt and traumas from this life, but also past lives that trigger this unresolved pain. So I feel Alf chose in his soul contract to resurrect all this trauma again, so that ultimately it could be understood and released. He chose to manifest the cancer and heart-breaking circumstances of his passing, which triggered

55

this reaction deep within your body. The ovaries are the point of creation for the female, so it's so interesting that this is where your cancer occurred - also in both sides as your feminine and masculine etheric bodies were somehow trying to find balance and make sense of all the stored trauma deep within your DNA.

Christo

Such a strong, loving soul, carrying so much wisdom and compassion for you. It feels like it was a long wait until you could be reunited. He has had other past lives which have enhanced his healing from that awful shared one with you. He was a constant monitor of your energies and worried about the dynamics between your husband and you. He took on so much of your hurt and disappointment of the failure of this marriage, especially after the happy expectations at the beginning. I said both men feel that they have to heal their shame of the desecration. I'm being shown the mountain of buffalo skulls depicting the carnage and depletion of the great herds and the native tribes that were eradicated. Their karma was to come into your lives again, to somehow work things through, but the triggers deep inside of you and their emotional blocks, prevented this from happening sadly - however as I said we can work with their higher selves, to see if they are now ready! I do feel from the animals, that this is what this life is all about! Sadly many of you have had to endure the physical manifestation of these traumas.

So Christo did his best to counter balance this. He was always there as your rock when things began to unravel in your relationship. I see him symbolically as a tall proud ship rolling and rebalancing on large waves of emotion, that were blowing through your home! I can see him nuzzling you around your sacral area as though he was aware of the cell activation brewing there - he did his best to take this on for you. Without him I think things could have been a lot worse for you - but as you say I think the healing he gave you kept the tumour enclosed, as though it was his way of 'holding' the energy of the trauma induced tumour to be contained.

I totally agree with what you were told about Christo choosing to pass at the time when you were unable to have control of this. He really needed to return to spirit where he was able to direct everything more and to orchestrate the return of the other soul beings back into your life - especially helping you to find Balu. I do feel that Christo has been a bear in another past life which is why his energy made you call him that! The other blessing (if you can call it that!) is the way that Capri was able to find his way back to you just after your operation! I feel that the left and then right leg injuries, were again so connected to the left and then right tumours in your body. I feel that the way it had spread then, was again indicative of the uncontained trauma energies as Christo had been unable to continue his restraint of the energies. Capri was somehow trying to be the one to balance things to relieve Christo from this duty somehow, as I'm sure that Capri was well aware of Christo's struggle.

His injuries were all about trying to carry the weight of responsibility that he had taken on for the soul family group - a mighty weight indeed! It was also about somehow helping you to find balance in your masculine and feminine (the left side is the feminine and the right the masculine, as you probably know!) I feel such a loving bond with Capri - such a beautiful spirit horse. I feel that Capri as a small calf, somehow managed to survive the massacre - something about the realisation on a soul level, of the barbarism of the destruction of Raven as the great white bull, pulled at your second husband's conscience. I feel your first   husband was the one who shot the fatal bullet to kill him. I feel that your second husband after the initial thrill of the blood lust came to his senses and called a halt to the massacre. I can see Capri; as such a tiny calf, tucked in between many huge mothers and other young males that he went unnoticed, but of course witnessed the massacre, but also carried the strong and sacred genes of Raven who could only reincarnate after Capri this time, when the circumstances were right for the traumas to be finally healed.

As young calves, you would probably have played together in happier times. It may be that Capri's mother was one of the *other horses that are in your lives - maybe Latin Love actually! Like I said this is the first opportunity for you ALL to get together to bring closure on this tragedy! I feel this is why seeing the video of Raven was so emotional for you as it reconnected you at a soul level after all this time!*

How does Clara get on with her father? Not sure whether it would be wise to tell her about the massacre which he contributed to - she might not be open to understanding that we all choose our life paths in order to experience and learn from them - not to attribute blame necessarily, just to work out how to grow from all our soul experiences.

I feel Clara also has the chance now to truly find herself and any emotional traumas that she is holding onto also will benefit from the re-write as the massacre seems to be the root cause of so much for you all!

Balu *was sent to you by Christo. He knew that you really needed the unconditional love that only a dog can give. Christo orchestrated everything. Balu was also killed in the massacre, but both he and Christo chose to be dogs rather than horses or people, so that they could be your constant monitors - I know that you spend a lot of time with the horses, but dogs are more our constant companions. I think it's very significant that Balu is so frightened of being left in the car, except when he's at the stables. I feel this is because he is more frightened of not being able to monitor you when you leave him, rather than frightened for himself - he feels unable to be in control of the situation, as because of the cell stored trauma, he is always in fear of something really bad happening again. When he is at the stables, he knows that you are with your soul family again and he can be calmer in that knowledge!*

I also think it's very significant that Raven has started to run backwards! To me this is showing me that he needs to return to the past to let go of his fears. As leader of the herd it was terrible for him to be dying and feel that he was unable to keep his herd safe and also to be the sacred wisdom keeper for the tribes. He is a huge power house, but due to his past he has

58

such deep rooted fears, which also escalate and circulate between you, Balu and him! So in a way you are all feeding each other's fears - however by running back to the past, he is showing you that this is where the answers lie. He is frightened to go forwards because he fears what might lie ahead - the past has been particularly traumatic, so goodness knows what the future might bring! He also picks up on your concerns about your future health of course which is only natural!

Balu really wants to be able to have fun and to lighten up - inside of this fearful dog is such a strong happy dog, if he could only allow himself to be free of the weight of this grief. So by creating a new story, we can help so many of your soul family on so many different levels. I feel sure that this will help you all now and those that have passed and now reside in spirit, guiding you towards this goal, so the next incarnations can be lovely free happy ones! We need you to be happy and healthy, so that perhaps Capri and Christo can find their way back to you again in this life! They played their part in getting you to where you are today right at this moment in time!

I feel you have a wonderful stellar past connection, who chose to incarnate in many challenging roles to experience the raft of emotions that humans and animals feel, in order to better under-stand how to heal them when you yourself are healed. This is why you are here and why you have endured so much. It's about your soul growth in order to help others understand that once the root cause is addressed, so much wonderful healing can take place. Your message to others is that if you can come through it then so can they!

You are a way shower - a guiding light! You have so much support from the animals and they honour your journey, as they know you will be their spokesperson to share the importance of listening to the animal kingdom and their profound messages for us - if we do not then there is little hope for the human race, or our beloved planet. The animals tell me we have reached a tipping point where there is salvation for us, but only if we start listening to the animals who know how to help us help ourselves! This is why animal communication is so important for us now. You will be one of the light bearers, with the help of your animals, to bring this knowledge to as many people as you can. This is your mission, so you have to be healed in order to carry out your duties!!

So let me know how this resonates with you - when you feel ready, we can book in a session for you to re-write the story and create a whole new dimension where it never happened, so all of you can be free of the weight of those awful cell memories! It's interesting that I didn't get so much about each individual - more about their combined journeys and how entwined you all are in the story and also the healing and restoration of it all, so that you can all go forwards in joy!

Let me know your thoughts - I do hope this makes sense to you - I can only give you what I am given, but the images were incredibly vivid and came through strongly as though I was watching a Technicolor movie!

Very best wishes
Madeleine

Anabell's reply

(I suggested Anabell work with the healing pyramid visualisation, which is included in the last chapter - she includes the healing effect it had in this response).

What I wanted to tell you;
On Friday evening I was so desperate I went into the forest in Betzdorf where I have a wonderful tree which gave me strength for quite some time already. When I leant my hands against it, my belly started to spin around intensively, first left side, then right side, this continued for quite some time, always changing directions left and right until it stopped. Then I felt something pulling my belly towards the tree, I stood like this for quite some time. After some time passed, I felt so light in my belly as if something has been torn out and disappeared through the branches towards the sky. I was so amazed when you wrote

about the pyramid spinning around, because this was just the same as I experienced it at the tree. I was there this morning again, it happened again, but only three times directions changed and the spinning was by far not that intensive as it had been on Friday. Life is so amazing. And when I imagine being in the pyramid, I started in a position like an embryo. After some sessions I knelt and since last night I am standing upright in it, looking up into the sky and a very bright light, I open my arms to the sky. I am wearing a white dress which is flying as if a strong wind blew into it and since this morning, Capri is beside me, looking in the same direction, standing very close to me and touching my hair with her mouth, softly blowing into my hair when she exhales. It is such a magnificent experience; I am deeply touched by it. I thank you for all this; I can hardly find words how thankful I am.

My reply;

Hi that's really wonderful! We have done some lovely healing on you tonight and you are wrapped still inside your pyramid, but around that is a wonderful crystal structure with prisms of rainbow light going through you and the tumours etc... The pyramid was spinning in one direction, removing all negative conditioning and then spinning in the other direction filling you with light so I really hope it helps!!

I have put you inside a beautiful etheric quartz healing pyramid. Imagine that you are sitting in there in a place of complete peace and breathe that peace into your whole body - especially the areas affected by the tumours and the issues with your intestines. Keep imagining yourself in there as much as you can and just breathe in that peace and also love and gratitude for your body!! Speak to those parts and see what they have to say - ask them what they need to be fully whole and healed and listen to their answers! I will be doing a concerted healing on you on Sunday evening with my friend to see what we can do for you! Hang on in there.

BIG love to you

More news from Anabell!

Soul Healing and Right Track for Life after Madeleine's Reading

I got into contact with Madeleine's work by reading her book about animals helping people to heal in the German translation. I was deeply touched and impressed by the book and the stories of healing and reincarnation and decided to contact her.

I always felt a deep connection to animals, had a dog and a cat in my childhood, and dogs after I settled down with my second husband. Unfortunately, both marriages of mine had been divorced. From the first husband I have a daughter, but no child with my second husband. Both separations had been accompanied by terrible wars of roses, both husbands having tried to destroy me completely. Twice I had suffered from ovarian cancer. When waking up from my first surgery in 2004, I was filled with a deep passion for horses, which I didn't have before. Following my passion, two years later I found my first horse, a wonderful Lipizzaner gelding. Further on five more horses found their way to me as well as after the death of my first Rottweiler, a second one which is still living with me. Two of the horses moved on to different people, but I can still see them as they are close to me. My first horse died four years ago. When I contacted Madeleine I lived with my second Rottweiler and two horses.

I told Madeleine about my sicknesses and animals and asked her to make a reading for me to see how I am connected to my animals and if we had been together in earlier lives.

It was amazing what Madeleine found out:

She told me that all of us, my animals, my daughter, my two husbands and myself had met in a former life in America. My animals, my daughter and I had all been members of a wild buffalo herd with a white bull, being the sacred master of the herd. My former husbands were white men, who had been hunting the herd and decimated it with no comprehension of what this meant for their souls and the souls of the animals. My actual Lipizzaner gelding, a pure white horse, was the white bull and my first dog in childhood, was my buffalo mother. Even my cat which I had in early childhood, was one of the buffaloes that life before. We all had found our way to each other this lifetime to heal the trauma we suffered and to be released and forgiven. Unfortunately at the time of meeting each other, my husbands and I were not yet ready to be healed or forgiven. But Madeleine proposed to do a re-write of the story, to create a new story and thus help our soul family to heal.

Even though it might sound strange for others to hear such a story of a buffalo herd in America, but my reaction showed me that deep inside I knew it was true. I felt a strong push in my heart region; I needed to get out of the house into the forest which begins right behind my backyard. I walked and walked, holding my breath, then breathing deep and all of a sudden I started crying, tears ran down my face and for minutes I wasn't able to get hold of them. I cried, I shouted, I ran. I knew it was true, I found the deep connection to my animals and my daughter.

Some weeks later Madeleine and I did the re-write in a skype session. Madeleine guided me, asked me what I saw. I was very excited, as this was done in English and I was worrying if I was able to find the words to describe what I could see and feel. But amazingly this was so easy, words came out easily. When I closed my eyes, I saw a beautiful valley, and a wonderful buffalo herd. We re-wrote the story, my second husband refraining from his intention to kill the buffalo, but instead helping them to escape from this slaughter. This made my first husband very upset. He didn't want to refrain from his plan to shoot the buffalo and started fighting with my second husband. Unfortunately my first husband was not able or willing to change his attitude - in contrast to my second husband - so we couldn't help his soul to be forgiven by the re-write at this time.

A week after the re-write I received a telephone call, showing the number of my second husband. Until that time, we didn't have contact with each other. In this terrible war of roses, he had tried to destroy my job and financial situation. First I was shocked to see his number... of course I didn't answer the phone, as I was scared of a new attack coming from him. Then after two days my feelings changed completely: I thought of the re-write, which also seemed to help me to forgive him. I decided to call him back and was amazed about his reaction. He told me that he had thought a lot about the times we spent together (more than 10 years) and he wanted to tell me that he is really very sorry for what he did to me. He wanted me to know that he really loved me and was happy that we spent the time together, he would never forget again. Now he is married again and from time to time we talk over the phone, with no bad emotions. I really feel that healing has taken place and that we can communicate with each other on a different level of friendship even.

Two months later I met my first husband at the graduation party of our daughter. As had been shown in the re-write, sadly he was not willing to let healing take place. My efforts to reach an amicable contact with him were not successful. But what was amazing for me was the perception, that I myself was able to have peaceful emotions for him. I had always been scared of him and contact with him, but these fears were completely gone. I felt easy in this contact and noticed that no negative feelings were reaching my heart any more.

Since my passion for horses had arisen, it had always been my dream to live together with horses, finding a house or farm with a stable and enough land for my horses and me to live. One month after the re-write I was offered an interesting place, a house with three hectares of land and a stable for horses, to buy. This house was close to my girlfriend, who had bought the first pony, Desirée, from my daughter for her daughter five years ago. The house was only 500 m away from the stable in which Desirée lives now. I was deeply impressed by the place, immediately found emotional connection and was deeply touched. One day, when I talked to a neighbour that I was thinking about buying the house, he said: "Well, if you really think about moving here you should know that this valley is called "buffalo valley" by the native people here and people might be pig-headed fellows." "It was as if I got struck with a hammer and knew, I need to move here with all my animals to finally find healing in our "buffalo valley" and what is amazing too, people in "buffalo valley" are not pig-headed at all… they are the nicest people I ever met in this lifetime!

Thank you, Madeleine, you helped me heal my life and showed me the right track!

Anabell continues to improve in her new beautiful home in Buffalo Valley! All the animals are also thriving - what an amazing story!

Jenny and Biscuit

Jenny and her partner Dave brought Biscuit, their dog to see me, as they were worried about Biscuit's aggressive behaviour. He was extremely nervous if anyone reached down to pat him on his head. The result would be that Biscuit would fly at them, trying to bite their hand. He was such a dear little dog and I could tell that he really wasn't aggressive, just fearful. He was a rescue dog and he showed me that he had been cuffed around his head regularly for minor misdemeanours as a pup in his early life - such as house training, but instead of positive reinforcement and praise, he would only receive a swipe to his head. I felt that his aura was 'dented' around his head, where he had stored the energetic memory of the blows and so if anyone penetrated his auric field, it would trigger the old fear and naturally cause him to react. So my first job was to remove the negative energy from his aura - almost imagining something like a dented car panel being gently knocked out, so the panel could be smooth and perfect once more! I then visualised him wrapped in a beautiful rose quartz crystal heart, as though he was sitting in the middle of it. I really hoped this would help release his fear and the anticipation of pain when anyone just wanted to pet him and show him kindness. However, when Jenny started to also tell me a little about her story and how Biscuit came to be with her, I started to see a bigger picture that was affecting them all.

Jenny had been a professional singer for a number of years, accompanied by Dave in their band. Unfortunately Jenny had always found performing in public very nerve wracking, so much so, that she had been forced to give up her singing career because of crippling panic attacks. Dave her partner, also mentioned that he had a lot of trouble with his painful left shoulder, which never seemed to completely go away.

I started to see a picture of Jenny on a platform speaking out for people in her community that she cared about, raising awareness of their plight. I could see Dave there and also Biscuit, but this time he was a young lad - a younger brother to Jenny. I felt that Dave was their older brother. This was connected to the Jarrow March and the terrible poverty and unemployment of Jarrow back in the 1930s. Although the concept might have seemed very strange to Jenny and Dave, I asked Jenny if she could visualise seeing herself back in that time and if so what she might be wearing and what her name might be. To her great surprise she could describe her red hair and green clothes that she was wearing. Dave could also see what they looked like back in that time.

Jenny also described a dream that she had had where she had been imprisoned unjustly, and that she had felt a huge sadness and feeling of guilt connected to the situation, but she didn't know why. I could see that Jenny and the crowd listening to her were attacked as the peaceful demonstration was disrupted by hired thugs and so the authorities retaliated. Dave was severely beaten with what looked like an iron bar, hitting his shoulder and head. Jenny was dragged off her platform and thrown into prison, whilst the young brother, Biscuit was abandoned and lost in the melee. It seemed to Jenny that because she had been the one to call the meeting and speak up for her community, it had been her fault that this terrible outcome had happened. I felt that Dave had died of his injuries and Biscuit had never been reunited with Jenny once she was finally released from jail.

The interesting thing that came up with this past life was that Jenny said that she was never fearful of the actual singing as she performed, only of the speaking in between the songs - as though speaking on a stage would somehow create a really bad situation, but not knowing what that could be. This was the trigger for her panic attacks. Whilst we were working through this past trauma, Jenny's throat had started to constrict, which was a reaction that had constantly affected her in the past and even in previous counselling sessions, when she was asked to feel into where she felt the fear in her body. I thought this was so significant, as it had been the 'speaking' that had created the situation for the terrible past outcome to happen. Jenny also said that she had always felt so protective of Biscuit and had this awful fear that she would lose him - also some deep rooted fear about something dire happening to Dave that would be her fault somehow. She also said that as a child, she had always been the quiet one, never wanting to speak up or put herself 'out there'. It was only because her voice was so beautiful, that she was constantly pushed beyond her comfort zone, being forced in a way to perform which had been a constant struggle for her. Until in adulthood the fear had got so bad she just stopped, as she could no longer put herself through so much stress.

It's so amazing how these deep rooted fears impact on us in our everyday lives and once we can understand where they come from, they can lose their power over us and so be released!

So with Biscuit's help, we created a whole new script, where the traumas never happened. I suggested to Jenny that she could imagine her really helping the people get better lives and how she was respected and recognised for her eloquence and passion to create better conditions for her community etc... Also that she and her brothers were all together living out fulfilling and safe lives. I encouraged her to keep going forward in a new timeline, seeing what a wonderful life that she had, rewarded for her commitment to the underdog and how Biscuit and

Dave also led safe and fulling lives.

As Jenny kept visualising the new story, her throat began to relax and Biscuit did some huge yawns, as though releasing the entire past trauma. It was amazing how everything from Jenny's current life's challenges, seemed to make sense once she understood where all her fear, guilt and sadness came from. Only allowing the new safe, happy memories to impact on her cell memories, could create a far happier life from now on. It was also amazing to realise how hard Biscuit had worked and struggled to find his way back to her in this life, having endured such harsh treatment, so that he would run away, be rescued and then seen on the rescue site by Jenny and of course destined to be homed by her, so they could all reunite to heal this terrible past trauma together! Jenny sent me an email later with some information from some research she had done about the whole Jarrow situation and she found some about a woman called Ellen, who she could really identify and resonate with. Whether she actually was Ellen or someone close to her at that time - the comparisons to what Jenny saw in this past life are certainly interesting. She had mentioned green clothes that she could see herself wearing and long red hair. You can see Jenny's comments within the text…

Ellen Cicely Wilkinson
Born: 8 October 1891 in Chorlton Medlock,
Manchester, UK
Died: 6 February 1947 (aged 55)
at St Mary's Hospital, London

Ellen Cicely Wilkinson was a British Labour Party politician who served as Minister of Education from July 1945 until her death. Earlier in her career, as the Member of Parliament (MP) for Jarrow she became a national figure when she figured prominently in the 1936 Jarrow March of the town's unemployed to London, to petition for the right to work. Although unsuccessful at that time, the march provided an iconic image for the 1930s, and helped to form post - Second World War attitudes to unemployment and social justice.

Ellen fought and won the municipal election of 1923 and became a Labour councillor. She was an exceedingly able speaker even in these early days and was particularly good at open air meetings. Her small figure, generally dressed in green (I SAID GREEN CLOTHES!) and her hatless flaming hair made a bright spot of colour in the drab Gorton streets.

Ellen Wilkinson the only woman and who led the Jarrow marchers whenever she could, made an impassioned plea to the Labour Party Conference in Edinburgh, and with tears streaming down her face, said: "Tell the Government, our people shall not starve!" …

On Saturday, October 31, the marchers finally reached London in heavy rain headed by Ellen Wilkinson leading the mascot dog, the town's Mayor and eleven councillors. Richard (Father) and Ellen (Mother) had four children.

Anne born in 1881, Richard born in 1883, Ellen Cicely in 1891 and Harold in 1899.

There was also a photograph showing the young Ellen (ME!) with her mother and her brothers Richard (Dave?) and Harold (Biscuit?) Clearly evident is the fiery red hair that became her trade mark. She inherited it from her maternal grandmother who had red hair long enough that she could sit on it. Ellen had ambitions to grow hers long too (I HAVE VERY LONG HAIR!) but eventually tired of it and had it cut short.

Soon after starting school Ellen became ill and, by her own account, would have died had it not been for, "a devoted and intelligent mother". She didn't return to school until she was eight and was taught at home.

There is a suggestion that this illness was a causal factor in Ellen's diminutive stature. She was a large baby but only grew to be 4 foot 10 inches as an adult. Wilkinson took up the cause of women's suffrage, the major women's rights issue of the day. Although initially engaged in everyday tasks such as distributing leaflets and putting up posters (THAT'S WHAT I DO NOW!). Wilkinson never married, (NEITHER HAVE I!) although she enjoyed numerous close friendships with men. Apart from her early engagement to Walton Newbold, she was close to John Jagger for many years, and in the early 1930s enjoyed a brief romantic attachment with Frank Horrabin.

Her long association with Morrison began in her early Fabian days; Morrison was very reticent about this friendship, choosing not to mention Wilkinson in his 1960 autobiography despite their close political association. Vernon says that the relationship almost certainly became "more than just platonic", but as Wilkinson's private papers were destroyed after her death, and Morrison maintained silence over the matter, the full nature and extent of their friendship remains unknown.

Wilkinson suffered for most of her life from bronchial asthma (EXPLAINS THE SORE THROAT AND COUGHING!!) which she aggravated over the years by heavy smoking and overwork. She had often been ill during the war, and had collapsed during a visit to Prague in 1946. The winter of 1946/47 was exceptionally cold and the ceremony was held out of doors. Shortly afterwards, Wilkinson developed pneumonia; on 3rd February, she was found in her London flat in a coma, and on 6th February 1947 she died in St Mary's Hospital, Paddington. At the inquest the coroner gave the cause of death as "heart failure" following emphysema with acute bronchitis and bronchial pneumonia accelerated by barbiturate poisoning". Wilkinson had been taking a combination of drugs for several months, to combat both her asthma and insomnia; the coroner believed she had inadvertently taken an overdose of barbiturates. (I HAVE A FEAR OF TAKING MEDICATION!) With no evidence to indicate that the overdose was deliberate, he recorded a verdict of accidental death. Despite this, speculation that Wilkinson had committed suicide has persisted; the reasons cited being the failure of her personal relationship with Morrison and her likely fate in a rumoured cabinet reshuffle. In their 1973 biography of Morrison, Bernard Donoughue and G. W. Jones suggest that, given Wilkinson's poor health, the burdens of her *ministerial office became too much for her. However, the lack of conclusive evidence divides historians about Wilkinson's intention to take her own life.*

I think you'll agree that Jenny had many similarities to Ellen and the way she felt when she read about her was really interesting, as well as how she identified herself in the old photograph, which unfortunately, we don't have permission to show.

You'll be pleased to hear that after all the healing that Biscuit facilitated and a session together, Jenny has now joined a fun local choir to be encouraged to get back into singing , just for pure pleasure, without any pressure at all, which is a huge first step for her - thank you Biscuit!!

Chapter 5

Self-Forgiveness…
Cetacean Soul Healing

Whilst swimming with a huge pod of spinner dolphins off Marsa Alam in the Red Sea, I was given a wonderful healing technique, to help people access very ancient programming that may impact physically and emotionally in their current life patterns and mind-sets.

The dolphins told me that many people found it very difficult to truly forgive themselves and love themselves unconditionally. They said that this was due to a kind of parasitic energy stored in their DNA, which prevented them really ever moving forwards, embracing their magnificence and fulfilling their true potentials. This could really limit their self-belief and create crippling lack of self-worth and never truly believing that they might deserve the very best their new life might have to offer them.

The dolphins spoke of many past lives in Lemuria and Atlantis, which people had experienced and still held much guilt about its downfall. Even outer planetary interference with their soul blueprints, as sometimes people were still carrying energy implants in their energy fields that were impacting on them physically and emotionally.

So the dolphins showed me how I could help people go back to the Atlantean healing temples and work with the healing tools there, to finally cleanse themselves of anything that no longer served them, or prevented them from being all that they were capable of, fully achieving all their heart's desires.

It has been a fascinating journey, working with the dolphins, who come in so strongly to support me, when I use their technique. They often wrap a person in a beautiful bubble of light and protection, to support their journey into the past, to finally rid themselves of their energy impediments. There is a meditation at the end of the book, which enables people to journey back into Atlantis and the healing temples therein, but it has since evolved into a far more profound healing experience, which I will describe as follows…

The dolphins usually come in to surround a person with a beautiful bubble of light and protection, as though creating a safe place for their inner core being to gently float down and away from their human 'overcoat'. The dolphins guide this core essence of them, gently down through time and space, until they are guided to visualise touching down on a beautiful blue star shaped crystal, inside a crystal healing temple back in the time of Atlantis. All around them, they can visualise crystals, but these are special as they appear like clear quartz, but with an inner fire. I suggest to the person that they might imagine a small obelisk type crystal in front of them and this crystal can have different functions, and with their mind they can ask the crystal to scan their etheric body, to then create a holographic X-ray, to show any imbalances or implants, that have remained there through many lifetimes, restricting and limiting them emotionally and even physically. The hologram is then overlaid or superimposed, over their body and then if there are any areas that are felt should not be there, I can guide the person to ask the light crystal to change its function to create a laser, which can then burn away the negative area in whatever way that feels right to them. They are also encouraged to imagine drawing up the healing blue energy of the blue crystal beneath them, as though using a two pronged approach to healing and releasing these blocks. When they seem to have been cleared, the scanning process is repeated, until everything feels clear or released. Then thanking the light crystals, the dolphins can gently guide the person back up through time and space, in order to reunite with their human body and allow integration of the new healing bodies to fully be absorbed and assimilated, anchoring in the healing that has taken place.

Maybe the best way to illustrate this experience is to recount an amazing session with a lovely lady called Alice in her own words as follows …

"I live at Uluru, and whilst it is a magical place to visit, it can be a hard energy to live in. I have had a number of problems since I arrived here, and then my mum happened to go and visit a psychic and was so worried about me that she asked questions about me. What the psychic said was so unbelievably accurate that I felt I needed to listen to the other more obscure things that she said. (I am no stranger to obscure psychic messages due to a more unusual upbringing, but my level of scepticism is also unusually high. I will either believe everything or nothing) One of these things was that I had DNA implants in my body and would benefit from occasional sessions with a sympathetic counsellor. My mum is friends with Madeleine and suggested that I arrange a skype session with her, especially as I feel a deep connection to whales and the psychic suggested that the sound of whales would help to cure my implants. One problem of living remotely is bad internet so this ended up being a skype conversation with no pictures, but I am a very visual person and I think that this worked better for me as I was able to fully immerse myself into the images that Madeleine described.

I am not so sure what order these occurred in... Madeleine asked me to scan my body and see if I could see/ feel anything. I picked up on a blockage in my heart and my throat, but wasn't sure if I was imagining this, as I always know that I have blocks that I have worked on there. Madeleine said she could see the same and also something in my right ear. When I focused on this area, I saw what almost looked like a little yellow plastic trumpet. She explained that this was making me hear things wrong. I think at this point a dolphin came in to shatter this with some high frequency sound. I felt like I was in some kind of special room and there was a 3D image of myself that was easy to scan internally. I also felt whales swimming around me although there was no water. I found that this trumpet shape was connected deeper down inside me and it took some work to remove, but Madeleine has a Narwhal that she called upon which helped to pull it out of my ear.

I also felt as though there were sheets of metal in my chest that were stopping the connection to the rest of my body, which we worked on dissolving, but under these I found that there were flowers growing in dirt that needed to be pulled out through my throat and more dirt kept coming out followed by hundreds of brightly coloured balls that rolled all over the floor. I visualised these turning to light as they hit the ground.

The most significant part for me though, was going in to my heart. I have often been told I need to open my heart and have spent a lot of time working on this, but this session made me realise how closed it actually was. Being asked to visualise my heart, I saw a bright red looking heart shape, only with chains and a padlock. Madeleine asked if I needed help getting in and we laughed because I said I had an angle grinder to do the job! Once inside myself, it was filled with purple stalagmites, which actually felt good. It was like a little cave with good energy, but once inside there were many things to address. Madeleine asked me to look around and see if I could see anything. At first I saw hieroglyphs and then Aztec symbols, which really surprised me as I don't feel any connection to that culture. I then saw a waterhole in the corner and walked over to it. Looking into the water, I saw images of myself in many different lifetimes flashing through the reflections in the water. I am in a unique position that I remember some past lives and recognised people I had been. I saw myself passing a ruby to each person to put in their heart and at this point had some connection to my dad and felt I needed to give him a ruby, because he had failed at his mission on earth and would die soon. (I do not have a relationship with my dad, but the psychic had said that DNA implants in me were all related to my father and his ancestors). I think Madeleine asked me if there was anything else I wanted to clear and I came back to a childhood memory. As a child in this lifetime I had memories of being a young girl in Victorian times, locked in her room to die. I had odd thoughts about this as a child, because I often longed to go back to those times, even though I was alone and dying. Madeleine suggested that I needed to go back and make peace with myself, so I found myself back in that room, but visualised someone coming into see me, but I realised that it was not a person, but an angel in a human form. I have a connection with Archangel Michael and felt his presence there. Coming back into my heart I also felt the spirit of a cat I had had in childhood.

Madeleine then asked if I wanted to fill my heart with any beautiful things like flowers, but that didn't feel right and I soon found myself focusing on two rather odd things. As a small child I was obsessed with the idea that I had come from a green planet, and on that planet we had viewing portals (that looked a bit like bird baths) where we could look at earth. I found myself putting this is one in one corner and then I saw there was a dragon in the other corner. I have always had a deep connection to dragons, but felt that if I said there was a dragon, this would be wrong in some way, because they're not exactly considered the most sweet-natured of creatures, but when I told Madeleine this, she said that she was wondering when to introduce this, as she works with dragons. A dragon was a great image for me too because someone once said to me that the best way to open your heart was to visualise a burning flame in it, but a dragon is both protective and has a flame on its breath. So the dragon remained in my heart lighting, warming and expanding it to keep it open from now on.

Eventually it came time to leave this area and I actually saw a little red car ready to drive me out! We checked another scan once more, but it then seemed clear so it felt fine to journey back and integrate the healing that had taken place."

I think you'll agree this was a pretty amazing session and was so heart opening for Alice. Going inside your emotional heart and communicating with it, is a very powerful exercise. It's very revealing when you get an idea of what it's like inside and also what it might have to say to you.

The dolphins really wanted Alice to feel safe in opening her heart up, but some ancestral issues had to be healed

first and some healing with her father was really important, as there were aspects from her childhood that had made her close her heart down.

Imagery is such a powerful tool, and the subconscious always gives us exactly what we need to create the best possible healing solutions - I loved that she had the dragon in there and the little red car waiting to bring her back out, to then visualise how her heart had changed.

Our emotional hearts can take such a battering, so visualising what our emotional hearts can look like and what they might like to tell us, as we remove them from our heart centres, can tell us so much symbolically, as to the condition of our emotions. By imagining that we can shrink down and find that we have a tiny key to unlock a little door in our hearts, we can go inside and create all kinds of healing experiences - lighting candles, placing beautiful crystals, shining a big torch to illuminate any areas of darkness. We can also invite loved ones inside.

I had a lady who invited her inner child inside for some healing, where they finally integrated, becoming as one, which felt so good after many years and made my client feel so happy - she even brought her father and brother in to resolve very angry childhood challenges, and in doing so helped to heal all kinds of ancestral soul family issues.

It's a very gentle but powerful exercise and so revealing as to how and what we need to heal.

Alice continued to find her job in the tourism at Uluru challenging, but knows that she is meant to be there, but I felt that she had to work more with the indigenous peoples there and that she also had past life connections with them, which was actually the real reason why she had returned to that sacred site. She has now applied for other work there with the aboriginal people!

Nature is not a place to visit it is home
Gary Synder

PART 2

PLANETARY HEALING...
Gifts from the guardians of Gaia

Chapter 6

Walking Between Worlds....
Meet the Ancestors

A very strange visitor

Crash went my cat flap in the kitchen! It was pitch black in the middle of the night. Now wide awake from the sound, I sat bolt upright in bed and my first thought was 'oh no what has my cat brought in now?', as he was prone to bringing me 'gifts' that were not always welcome! Little was I to realise then just *how* much of a gift was coming into my kitchen that night in August. However, as I blearily tried to look around my room, I felt to my amazement that my cat was curled up fast asleep on my bed next to me - so *what* had come into my kitchen?

I leapt out of bed and went to investigate - only to hear the cat flap crash again, as whatever had been there had hastily made its exit. As I was going into the kitchen I thought oh it must be another cat trying to come in and steal some food, but when I saw the size of the damp paw prints on the floor, I was alarmed at the size of them and thought… that must be a *big* cat! I decided to lock the cat flap from the inside, so that whatever it was could not come in and harm my cat, and then sleepily stumbled back to bed. An hour later I heard the cat flap crash open once again - now I was really alarmed at what might be desperately trying to get into my house and what it might do! I ran out of my bedroom, down the hall and into the kitchen and in my amazement, saw a large grey furry backside shoot back out of the cat flap. Somewhere in my drowsy state I had a tiny glimpse of its face and its stripy tail, which in the depths of my consciousness, I thought was very strange, but only allowed my conscious mind to register that it could only make sense that it must have been a badger! My dog's water bowl was full of grass and mud, which again I thought was weird and also that it would be very unusual for a badger - normally a very shy creature, to come into someone's house, but I surmised it must just be very hungry or thirsty.

So I thought I'd sort it out in the morning, by putting out some food and water for it. This I did for several nights, but my visitor seemed determined to continue to trash my cat flap and come into my house at varying intervals during the following nights.

Finally I asked the question why? To which I 'heard' an exasperated "At last!" What I *thought* was a badger, started to 'download' the most incredible messages to me, usually at around 4am in the morning, forcing me to wake up and scribble down very surprising words, many of which made no sense to me at all. I wasn't even aware of how to spell some of the words that he was formulating in my mind! Sometimes it took the form of a two way conversation, where I could ask questions, other times he would just convey the odd sentence or incredible one liner! I say he has. I had decided to name him Brock, which is a kind of nickname given to badgers in the UK. This continued for several nights, but then the visits seemed to stop, but the messages continued to pour into my mind in our early morning communications! I also noticed that the food I'd been putting out for him was suddenly not being eaten, and I was a little sad that he might have moved on to visit someone else. I'd made sure that my cat was safe with me at night and due to the incredible messages coming through thick and fast, I really hoped that I might get to see him physically again. This was not to be then, as I heard on the local news that a very surprising creature had been captured in my road, by the local badger rescue centre.

Apparently I wasn't the only person to have been surprised by this nocturnal visitor, he had also been creating chaos in another garden, by rolling their flower pots around - My neighbours had also thought it was a badger, as what else could a grey, stripy, fluffy creature be in the British countryside?

Much to the astonishment of the badger rescue people, when they arrived to see what they had captured in their trap, they saw a large raccoon! If this had happened in North America, where I have seen many raccoons, I would have understood it, but we don't have raccoons in the UK! Brock was found to be wearing a red collar, so had obviously been someone's illegal pet who had been dumped in fields nearby.

So not only did I have to realise that I'd had a raccoon in my house, which as I said would be weird enough to explain to anyone else here in England, but the subject matter of his 'downloads' to me were completely off the scale crazy, and that I would have to find a very special person to relay them to! I began to realise, the messages that continued to come through, were really important for me to share with people who would understand them and not only that, but to make use of his information, as it was several feet over my un-scientific head! I knew it was important in understanding more about our beautiful planet and our universe.

The following passages are some of his 'downloads'. I was fascinated, when I did a bit of research, to find that much of what he was saying was making sense when he talked of Cosmology and Quantum physics! I couldn't believe that a raccoon had gone to so much trouble to find me and then 'tell' me all this information. I felt compelled to try and discover more and to share it. I felt this was a whole new dimension in the healing and teachings of animals for humankind.

I looked into his revelations about Orgone energy, which I had never heard of, and was amazed to find so much information about its healing potential and the work previously done using healing chambers etc... by Wilhelm

Reich an Austrian Psychiatrist in the 1930s. He discovered this form of energy, which he saw as blue in colour, which he named Orgone energy or universal life energy.

He invented Orgone Accumulators to extract the Orgone energy from the ether and used it to treat many conditions including cancer. However, the US FDA (food and drug administration) tried to stop him, stating that Orgone didn't exist and ordered all his equipment and books to be destroyed. Quantum physicists have now proved that it does exist and the devices that Reich invented in accumulating and transmuting energy, so called dead Orgone radiation into balanced positive Orgone radiation energy, could work. Modern day generators have been used to neutralise electro-magnetic radiation from cell phones, computers etc... It is also now believed that a deficit in the body's positive Orgone energy flow is the main cause of physical dis-ease and emotional imbalances. It is our life force - our Chi! Here are some of Brock's messages in chronological order;

Brock's Wisdom
20.8.12 Orgone Energy

Brock: *"The ancient tribes believed in the concept of the - Orgone Alchemy - the changing of matter and energy. This is soul alchemy, it is found in the frequencies (sounds) of cetaceans and the vibrations of sacred geometry i.e. pyramid structures etc., it is a silent invisible force. The alchemy of the soul - you have been imbued with this energy when the sounds of the whales and dolphins have permeated your body. You must share this knowledge again, as it has been dismissed and forgotten - it is a gift from the animal kingdom, connected to the 'God particle'. It is the purest form of love.*

Madeleine: *"What can you tell me about how I can help the plight of the badgers in the proposed cull?"* I was very concerned about the imminent government planned cull of these beautiful creatures - I was astounded at what Brock said the badgers were trying to do!

Brock: *"Regarding the badger's plight of the culls connected with Bovine Tuberculosis - the badgers have chosen to be infected in order to transmute the virus and protect the cattle in the future."*

I tried to see if anyone could get a blood sample from an infected badger to see if indeed the virus was being mutated, but I couldn't find anyone who would help with this.

22.8.12
Brock: *"The quotient ratio is equal to the hypotenuse hypothesis of anti-matter"*

23.8.12
Brock: *"Sextant stars navigation amelioration logistics"*

27.8.12
Brock: *"S21 converging with S29 creating massed constellations. Geothermic land mass movement coincides with this convergence. 2x+y53 squared = 95billion to the power of 3. Lunar movement creating Orgonic sound waves turning the tides and patterns of light. A HARMONIC MOMENT IN FRACTAL TIME"*

29.8.12
Brock: *"GALACTIC IMPRINT"*

30.8.12
Brock: *"The binary codes are overridden by the tertiary congruent. These mediate triangulation of the stellar wave systems".*

01.9.12

Brock: *"The tertiary triangulation points coincide with the star nebulae to alter dimensions through Orion".*

Madeleine: *"Are these filtered through Orion gamma rays?"*

Brock: *"The gamma rays transmute dysfunctional energies and transmit pure light (Orgone) they are cleansers/purifiers, so that this pure energy can be allowed to pass through the atmosphere and into the earth and its inhabitants. The tertiary codes show the star nuclei radiate the gamma rays. All the nuclei in every atom of life are the same – we are all ONE"*

03.9.12

Brock: *"Speeding up of the sun's rotation causing centrifugal force and cause of flares to be expelled also connected to the shifting poles. The sun's axis is altered and sped up.*

04.9.12

Madeleine : *"Can you tell me anything about the lion grids within the earth?"* (I had heard about these grids and my love of lions made me curious!)

Brock: The Lion Grid ...OIL

"The lion grid running from Mesopotamia to Guadeloupe is fractured near the Suez Canal; this may have been damaged during the excavations having affected the energy lines there. This has created all the turmoil regarding ownership of oil. If we can help the lions repair this, order will be restored. Oil is the land mass' life force being drained away by humankind. It has given us the greatest advances and disputes globally. The earth offers up her bounty, but it has been abused. The North Sea oil coming from the sea bed is old land claimed by the ocean, monitored by the cetacean species coming into the area trying to bring balance, which is why there have been many more sightings of more diverse cetacean species around the coasts of Britain.

05.9.12

Brock: *"The tertiary waveband correlations sub-divide fractal* orbs. *Emissaries of light journey through these wavebands as portals, refracting orgonic light, expanding and ameliorating the healing to Mother Earth's vibrations that this brings.*

08.9.12
Brock: Star systems and cosmic movement
"Dark energy is the lubricant for dark matter to pass through the universes as they speed up and expand - for all matter to pass through - stars, planets, everything!"

10.09.12
Brock: Cosmic breath
"Dark energy is like the breath of the cosmos. However it's like the respiration rate is increasing and as the 'out breaths' lengthen, so the universes widen and expand further and further - almost like a regular pulse - a quickening... a living breathing entity. Each planet has its own heart beat and breath, aware of the bigger breath of the cosmos which is the life force behind them all - a myriad of star systems constellations, galaxies, universes, all dancing to the rhythm of the breath of dark energy"

19.09.12
Brock: Expansion and alignments
"The tertiary alignments of Saturn and Neptune, together with the configurations of Mars, create an un-precedented energy of expansion creating yet more universes, which will be more readily visible, bringing more awareness of the extent of galactic changes and the impact they have on the earth. More and more beings of light and emissaries are making themselves known through the crystal implants and inner networks of connecting crystalline energy systems and grids. Everything is being activated NOW!"

24.09.12
Brock: There are many dangers to the planet
"Through fracking, you humans are destroying the earth's structure, and this will only create adverse balance

within the earth, forcing shifts in the tectonic plates. You must go to the Solar Plexus earth chakra, I will guide you when you get there!

I think you'll agree this is pretty extraordinary information. When he was telling me about the need to visit the solar plexus earth chakra, I felt a terrible pain in my stomach, solar plexus area. Brock told me it was the pain of the planet, because of the disrespect of humanity to Mother Earth through their feelings of unworthiness and disconnection to our home. I had no knowledge as to where the solar plexus earth chakra was, so once again I researched it, only to find that it was at Uluru in Australia. What really gave me goose bumps was the fact that I was actually due to go there, at the time of the message, in about two weeks!

An Antipodean adventure

I had been invited to speak at a big annual animal conference in Wellington New Zealand, in order to lecture about the profound connections between animals and humans, which I had discovered in my work. I wasn't sure how it might be received, as I had noted that there were a number of quite conventional speakers, who would be discussing statistics and more slightly main-stream topics! However, my lovely cat Thebes who I've mentioned before, had died a year before, and had told me that he would always be there to guide me from spirit in the next levels of my work, 'told' me exactly how to present my important message!

I only had a few days in New Zealand, before doing a two week stopover in Australia, where a friend had booked flights for us to go to Uluru! Before leaving Wellington, I had one free morning, so with a new found friend from the conference, we visited downtown Wellington, and went to the Te Aro Pa visitor centre, which houses remnants of an ancient Māori pa or village, dating back to the mid-1800s.   It was unearthed in 2005 during the construction of a new central city apartment complex. I had no knowledge of this when I visited, but was drawn to enter a beautiful ceremonial hall within the centre. Even though it was the school holidays and the rest of the centre was packed with tourists, this part was completely deserted, which was just as well when what followed occurred! As I stood in the middle of the beautiful hall surrounded by Maori carvings and designs, I felt a very strong presence behind me, almost forcing me to lie down. I felt I had to surrender in order to appreciate what I needed to learn from this experience. I had previously strongly felt that I would somehow reconnect with the Maori elders, which was one of the reasons for my visit to this part of the world! I was guided to lie in a foetal position. I suddenly felt surrounded by spirit ancestral Maori tribesmen, who told me I was experiencing a rebirth into my crone wisdom. I even felt strong painful contractions around my body, as though I was being pushed out of a birth canal. I could feel spiral tattoos appearing on my face and my skeleton changing into more crystalline structures, in tune with the earth's inner crystal network. I was told that I was a 'walker' between worlds, who had to learn information from the ancestors, human and animal, and to share their wisdom. This was my mission and I had to agree to it!

Of course I agreed, and now feel so privileged to be this 'traveller', so that I can now share this information with you. All this was in preparation for my journey to Uluru, where I knew there would be other ancestral aboriginal elders waiting to guide me.

I was excited as to how Brock would assist me to bring healing to the planet, when I reached the iconic huge red rock!   My friend and I started to walk around the enormous red stone walls that towered above us. Suddenly I felt Brock's presence with me and I was guided to stop at an exact location in order to do my work. He guided me to visualize implanting three huge etheric crystals. These can take form in many different shapes and colours. I have used them in my healing work for many years, which is a throwback to my ancient knowledge from my lifetimes in Atlantis, which many of you will have had. This is why so many people are fascinated in finding its true location and understanding its legends. The first crystal was a rose pink diamond shape, which I intuited would fit perfectly into a huge water crater within the surface of the rock, which led into a massive chasm. This was to purify and could only be felt and accessed by those who were pure of heart. The second was a huge blue pillar, which was a very strange long geometric shape, but fitted perfectly into a matching shaped fissure. The final crystal was an enormous silver/purple disc that was a transmitter, as well as a receiver. The rain water would take the healing energies of the crystal down into the earth. I could feel the presence of the aboriginal elders everywhere, standing poised on one leg, leaning on their spears, with their wonderfully sculptured features smiling at me. They gave me another surprising message in that they told me that the 'big birds' in the sky came down and took five children to impregnate, in order to bring the ancient 'future' knowledge back. They told me this future knowledge is sent by the Pleiadians. There are many people nowadays that believe that we originate from the star beings and that there are many coming to us now, to help us heal ourselves in order to protect the future of earth. I was then guided to walk the entire base of the rock, which was quite arduous, as by then it had begun to get dark. Luckily my friend had a head torch, but it was a little unnerving to see all the eyes of many dingoes around us.

I felt they were monitoring our progress and that we had to circumnavigate the base in order to anchor in the healing energies that I'd facilitated.   The next day I felt drawn to visit the extraordinary rock formations of the

Olgas or Kata Tjuta, which were very close to Uluru. About ten years before I had experienced an incredibly

powerful meditation, where I had entered a cave and found an ancient looking aboriginal man who said his name was Old John. He seemed to welcome me with so much love and I felt that I had finally come home and was exactly where I needed to be, enveloped in the love of my tribe. I'd had so much resistance to coming back from that meditation, as it seemed that that was where I was meant to be and that there hadn't always felt so much love in my current reality! It took me so long to be fully grounded and present after the meditation, and I always hoped that if I ever got the chance to go to Australia, I might physically meet Old John!

So when I got to the Olgas, I could see there were many cave like formations in the rock walls and I hoped that perhaps I would find the one from my meditation.

However, I suddenly felt an energy presence near me and I sensed that the wonderful elder was there stretching out his hand, as though beckoning me to walk through a rock passageway, into the most beautiful amphi-theater type canyon, where he said we would have to perform a sound ceremony. He told me that the ancient Jidhara people were given light crystals from the star people. They called them moon stones because they reflected the moonlight. When the Jidhara people were persecuted by the white men, they buried the crystals, so that the white people could not abuse the crystal's power. So many aboriginals were killed, that there was no one left who could remember where the crystals had been buried, or indeed how to use them. These crystals were conductors of healing energy for the earth and its indigenous people who were in tune with the beauty of the earth. John told me that the long buried crystals had been 'turned off' and needed to be reactivated now in order to help re-empower the earth and its inhabitants. He said that they were inverted now so that their energy would be directed deep into the earth, like a crystal network, or mycelium of crystal threads connecting the inner earth structures. We felt enormous energies shifting within the canyon, as we were guided to tone and give voice, as the incredible acoustics resonated and reverberated around the rock formations.

I hoped that I was performing the correct procedures in assisting John with this planetary healing. It felt incredibly powerful and we felt very emotional. The biggest Goanna appeared as soon as we felt we had completed our task, flicking his tongue at us as though feeling the energies and I thanked him for helping me perform my duty!

I had one day left in this beautiful area and we decided to drive to Kings Canyon. The universe and Brock, had orchestrated so many synchronicities and serendipitous events, which only afterwards were fully appreciated. Just one of them being on arrival at the Ayres Rock airport, our proposed hire car had not been returned in a good condition from its previous drivers, so the car hire company gave us a four wheel drive alternative, much to my delight, as it allowed us on this final day to be able to get to the last part of my healing mission!

As we were driving along the empty dusty road which seemed to go on eternally into the distance, I suddenly saw a huge rock formation which reminded me of Table Mountain. A huge flat topped mountain in the distance, only accessible by driving down a very rough dirt track, ideally suited to our off road vehicle, but would have been impossible in an ordinary car! The rock formation was called Mount Conner or Atula, which is what the aboriginals called it. I later discovered that the rock of Mount Conner is 200 to 300 million years older than the rock of nearby Uluru and Kata Tjuta. When we finally arrived near the huge gorge, feeling thoroughly bumped and rattled after the trek down the dirt road, I received further instructions from Brock. I was guided to implant a huge diamond shaped, multi-faceted clear quartz etheric crystal, into the mountain range. I had to visualize rotating it in order to connect with the other two sacred sites and their crystal network. I was told it was a sacred trilogy of sites that were now re-activated.

A beautiful hawk flew over us after I'd completed this earth healing and I fervently prayed that I had been of some assistance to our beautiful planet.

This was the message from Brock to me after I performed the healing at Uluru which is the Solar Plexus Earth Chakra.

08.10.12

Brock: *"The crystal mycelium is connecting and activating the inner structures that will strengthen the earth's resistance to fracking - cushioning the fragile fabric of Gaia. We can already see the effect as the earth takes a deep breath. The blue crystal is a direct conduit for the Orgone energy to reach deep down into the inner earth realms. The purple silver disc receives and transmits the moonstone energy safely, guarded by* *the pink diamond which deflects any dark controlling energies. The purity of the Orgone will counteract this. The solar plexus earth chakra is now a power house of pure crystalline energy - a Transmuter of the dark into light, further supported by the white diamond energies from Atula- a three pointed energy field - All is well! A facilitated amelioration of the corresponding stellar triangulation points!"*

I sat on the short flight back to Sydney faithfully recording this final message from Brock at that time. I hope that I had served him well and again marvelled at the timings and synchronicity of my amazing foreign visitor through my cat flap!

Working with Light crystals

I feel that we can all intuit these beautiful etheric crystals, if we feel drawn to bring healing to people, animals and our environments in this way. I believe every healing task that we perform, must always come from a place of loving intention and as long as we always ask permission from the recipient for the very highest good of all, we can't go far wrong. I always call in the highest assistance from the ancestors to guide me; so that I feel reassured that I have the purest energies helping me. Many of you will have been fascinated by real crystals and may already use them in healing, as each one has its own remedial qualities. Working with the light crystals adds a whole new dimension in crystal healing, and I have seen amazing results when working with them. I close my eyes and focus on my open hand, inviting a crystal form to be placed there. They always arrive etherically, in the form and colour that will be most beneficial. They can be soft and malleable, flat, spiral, geometric in shape or in enormous formations, like the ones that appeared to me in Australia, which you can just gently intuit guiding and placing where you feel is right. Those of you, who feel drawn to working in this way, will have worked with the crystals in other lives, so know that you will remember how to use them if it's right for you to do so. You too can play your part in helping the earth and its inhabitants!

Chapter 7

Where Whales and Lions
Meet a Shamanic Home Coming

*You must talk to the whales at night, when they speak in their
language of a great coming together or animals and man*

Credo Mutwa

My love affair with whales started in 1992, when I was
invited to visit Vancouver, in order to celebrate the birthday of my then boyfriend. Little did I know that this trip
would affect me so profoundly and create such life
changing events and dictate the course of the rest of my
days from then on! I was to fall in love twice on this
adventure. One was to last a lifetime, the other sadly not.
My boyfriend and I decided to make this trip a honey-
moon, as we found someone who could marry us to
complete our whirlwind romance.

On this trip we visited the Vancouver Aquarium, which is
a marine science centre. At that time they had two captive
killer whales. Once standing by the glass wall of their
tank, I was completely transfixed and couldn't tear myself
away for ages. Even the lure of my new husband, could
not convince me to move!

One orca kept coming right up to the glass opening her
mouth, as though speaking and connecting with me. I
could feel my whole body vibrating, though at that time I
was still ignorant as to the effect the close proximity of a
cetacean could have. I pressed my face against the glass
feeling trancelike, as the orca sent waves of love into me.
For years I couldn't remember the names of the orca, until
I was in Hawaii, speaking at the Cetacean summit - such
was the extent of my journey with whales since that first
meeting, that I was invited to share my experiences and
encounters with the summit audience. I was seated in the

audience listening to the speaker before me, and I was recounting my first encounter and happened to say that I couldn't remember the orca's name, when the lady sitting next to me interrupted, apologising for eavesdropping, but said that she had worked at the Vancouver aquarium at that time and that she could tell me their names. The one I felt had interacted with me so profoundly was Bjossa, so when I stood to speak and recount my first encounter with a cetacean, I was able to tell people her name. The universe works in mysterious ways, as of all the people I could have been sitting next to, it had to be the person who could tell me that vital piece of information, so I could credit Bjossa with the gifts she had given me!

Sadly after twelve mostly happy years, my marriage failed. This was extremely heart-breaking for me, but I now realise that my relationship had only been for that finite time and was all part of the greater plan to lead me forwards to do the work of service I was contracted to perform for this life. I was later told by Bjossa, then in spirit, that she was an emissary of light, sent to activate me and others, during her ordeal of captivity although I do not condone cetacean captivity whatsoever, I do under-stand now how much these beautiful beings are affecting the humans that can come into contact with them. The story of Selena, the captive dolphin in my first book "An Exchange of Love", also illustrates this.

Their higher consciousness knows that they have, on this level, chosen to be these wonderful long suffering ambassadors of cetacean wisdom, to raise awareness and the human vibration, assisting in the ascension process. By being captive, many more humans can interact with them and be affected by them, than would be possible in the wild, however awful this seems. I wonder how my life would have been if I hadn't met Bjossa - I bless her heart with so much gratitude, thanking her commitment to humankind, beautiful orca light being, trapped in her captive body for many years until she returned to the light. The following are some of the cetacean adventures and sharing of wisdom that I have been blessed with, since my awakening by Bjossa.

The Whale Mothers speak

I said to myself "If I could see a blue whale just once, I would die happy!" I remember the TV footage of Sir David Attenborough, out at sea in a small boat and suddenly realising that the biggest creature on the planet was just swimming by! His normally calm, composed exterior, could not fail to show its total awe of the moment. I have been lucky enough to swim with several different kinds of whale and dolphin in their natural habitat... but to see a blue whale - that *would* be something!

My dream came true in February 2013. I'd flown into Loreto, Mexico and we had just one day to find these rare, elusive creatures. We'd spent the night in a great little hotel and our alarm clocks were set bright and early the next morning for our wonderful adventure which really was a chance of a lifetime.

I awoke very early, too excited to sleep, to just doze, meditating on the day ahead and what it might bring. In my half dream state, I felt a huge blue whale mother come into my being and speak to me. She said her name was Celestial Star and said *"I will make my presence felt today and you will feel it in your heart. There will be many of us in evidence, blowing in order to strengthen the earth's protective matrix further".* I had been told by the humpbacks, that every time the whales 'blow', the energy of their breath goes to reinforce a beautiful protective force field around our beloved planet. The next piece of information from the whale elaborated on this. *"We have the biggest lungs and therefore the biggest lung capacity of any living creature on the planet. We hold the divine breath to oxygenate the oceans, so all sea creatures can breathe. The standing people (trees), do this for* clearly and I was tingling from head to toe! I scribbled down her message and felt guided to keep it to myself, until I felt her presence in our physical reality, which I felt convinced was about to happen! She'd also shown me many dolphins swimming around with the whales and I couldn't quite believe that we would be so lucky to see both species within the next few hours.

The weather was flat calm, the most perfect conditions and we set out in our little boat, chugging away through the gentle sea swell. We laughed at the antics of the seals that honked at us as we passed. They appeared to dice with death as the waves seemed sure to crush them against the jagged rocks, but they would emerge once again frolicking and revelling in the fun of their foamy home. Suddenly our captain said he'd spotted something. The mammoth whale waited until we were almost upon it and then she dived. Her gigantic tail fluke glistened and sparkled in the light, as the water droplets drizzled back into the sea. The iconic image of a submerging whale tail sank effortlessly into the watery depths beneath us. We weren't sure if we'd actually really just seen a blue whale and I wondered if I was still dreaming! I had the same feelings of tingly awe as I'd felt in my bed. I then felt a huge surge to my heart and I knew it was the whale that had previously spoken to me. Just then lots of dolphins appeared, riding our bow wave, as though celebrating our great fortune. We were lucky enough to see four more blue whales, just to make sure that I'd had my wish granted!

The weather had been so kind to us, as the next day a terrific storm blew up and no-one could get out to see any blue whales for about a week. Our one day, one chance, had given us such an incredible experience and beautiful message to share, little did I realise barely a month later, that another iconic creature would also link in with the blue whale's messages, showing me yet more evidence of the animal kingdom's unity of co-guardianship of our

planet however, we had more cetacean encounters to bless us. We travelled across wild desert terrain by minibus to Baja, to the San Ignatio lagoon, to meet the grey whales and their calves. This beautiful area is a reserve for the whales to calve and allow their young to be big and strong enough to endure the exhausting rigours of their long migration to the feeding grounds of the north. We stayed at the eco resort, set up by the man who was formerly involved in whaling. In 1968, the whales appeared to be so trusting and friendly, it completely changed his whole attitude and he was the first person to work to create the reserve and work with conservationists to protect the whales and secure the future safety of their birthing place.

The strong winds that had whipped up in Loreto followed us down to the lagoon, so the first day we were unable to get out to meet the grey whales. But again I'd felt their presence when in bed, with the energy of the whales all around me. They downloaded information similar to the kind of messages Brock had shared with me. They told me "The binary codes are overridden by the tertiary frequencies!", but then a voice seemed to say to me "Welcome! All your lifetimes you experienced for us were to learn all the different human emotions - love, loss, grief, barbarism, joy and enlightenment - different sides of the coin" Again their energy was electrifying and I felt as though I'd been zapped through my whole system. I certainly felt as though I'd been on a long journey through time, experiencing many challenges along the way. It seemed that the whales were aware of this and wanted me to understand why I'd felt so challenged. I also felt that people needed to understand that their lifetime challenges weren't a punishment; they were just experiences to allow their soul to grow and evolve.

The whales wanted me to share this information and on our very last encounter, they seemed to save the best till last.

We'd had three days of wonderful weather and fabulous encounters, as the whale mothers brought their babies up to our boats to bless us with their presence. Often they would roll on their sides and peer at us with their soulful eyes, the babies inquisitively rubbing against us, allowing us to caress their faces, as we reached out from our little motor boat. One huge mother rolled on her back and proceeded to pass right under our boat as we rubbed her belly, her huge body seemed to go on forever! In the very last minutes or our final moments, the mother and her calf surfaced again right next to us and simultaneously blew from their blow holes, their breath wafted into our faces in a myriad of refracted rainbows in the water particles. I felt compelled to write these words when we arrived back on shore.

The Rainbow Breath
Sweetest spray caresses my face
As the sound of the blow emblazons my senses,
The huge being graces us with her divine breath.
I feel blessed to the core of my soul.

We sadly sailed back to shore saying farewell to the whales as they appeared with their young all around us. I

wished them safe passage on their imminent arduous journey and I prayed that the calves would be safe against the perils that awaited them.

The Sperm Wales of Dominica

As I mentioned I'd been lucky enough to swim with whales in different parts of the world. I'd joined a research group to record the sightings of the sperm whales off the coast of the island of Dominica. This pod has been monitored for several years now and it was so exciting to be allowed to swim with them. They are the biggest toothed creature on the planet and hunt giant squid at tremendous depths in the cavernous ocean offshore. A hydrophone amplified their special encoder clicks that they use as sonar and communication. They also use their sound to stun their prey. Even their young are huge and are born weighing several tons.

One 'baby' allowed me to swim right next to him, and momentarily made eye to eye contact with me. I felt the clicks resonating and fine tuning my body and the bubbles, coming up from the hunting party deep beneath me, danced around my body. This is the message that the whale gave me.

Sperm Whale Speak

"Our sound holds the rhythms of the universe. It was founded in Atlantis in the ancient times as the beginnings of verbalisation of thought forms and telepathic communication, expanded into everything having its own sound to express individuality. The bushmen of the Kalahari - an ancient tribe in the heartland of the stirrings of mankind, still retain the 'clicks' in their spoken words. The 'click' stream that you felt and absorbed, were

further fine tuning your being into remembering at a cellular level, all that you have temporarily forgotten and will aid you in reclaiming all that has been left unclaimed for eons of time - there is so much that has been let slip from your knowing, it is crucial that you access this knowledge at this time. When we had eye to eye contact, I looked deep into your being and I saw that your heart was ready and willing to take this wisdom forward at this time of expansion and inter-dimensional realities, in that you as a race have the choice to join in what the rest of the kingdoms know already. You have been limiting yourselves for too long now. NOW is the time to unify and work as one, re-attaching your selves to the life plan of Gaia. This is a time of great change and re-balance, and fear should NOT come into the equation. Allow the love that we create in the ocean depths and widths to spread into your psyche. Completion of your long journeys is at hand. Spread the frequencies of our sounds' energies wherever you go and tread into the memory of your path, both in the physical steps you make on the land, but also in the steps that you make in your re-awakening awareness. Your human lifetimes are but a blink in time, but there is much to achieve during your brief stay on the physical plain. Your challenge has been to find your way home to unity and love. Continue on your quest - there is so much more to come, but for now, we honour and appreciate your willingness to be of service and all the progress you have made. NEVER lose faith in our love for you; you are never alone in your endeavours. We are behind you every 'step' of your journey!"

All love and blessings and peace from the whale unity consciousness.

I felt that the whale was asking me to somehow find and connect with the Bushmen to be a bridge of unification between them. I wasn't sure how on earth I could do this, but then everything fell into place so that I could!

Return to the Homeland

This was the prelude to my next adventure after the blue and grey whale trip. I'd wondered how I might ever get to visit the Kalahari and the bushmen to hear their 'clicks', but the universe contrived to make this possible, just one month after my communications with the whales in Mexico. Not long after I'd booked the whale trip, I received an email about a wonderful experience to return to South Africa, which was a sacred pilgrimage back to the origins of man. There were three sections to the trip and each component filled me with excitement. The first part of the journey was to visit Credo Mutwa an incredible high Sanusi and Zulu shaman, author of many books on the origins of man and esoteric ancient knowledge. After reading about him in Linda Tucker's book *'The Mystery of the White Lions'*, and hearing her speak about her tutelage by the great man, I'd met her with the white lions in South Africa four years earlier, and afterwards, I'd always wanted to have the chance to meet him. He was ninety four years old and I knew that I had to take this opportunity to get to meet and learn from him.

Sitting in his house listening to his wisdom, sharing a meal with him and his lovely wife, seeing his incredible sculptures and paintings, was such a privilege and one that I will always treasure. The final day with Credo was so special. He created a naming ceremony, where we would all receive our Zulu names. I hadn't really spoken much about my experiences with the ocean creatures, but he knew exactly what to call me!

Nowandle (pronounced Nowaandlay) which means daughter of the sea – a mermaid! I felt so honoured and profoundly blessed to have the opportunity to spend time with this magnificent wise man. His messages to us still ring in my ears.

"You must have dreams - a person without a dream is like a dog with a heavy collar - weighed down with no freedom. You must talk to the whales at night, when they speak in their language of a great coming together of animals and man. Let us listen to the stories that are given to us when we dream.

105

Animals and human beings are intertwined by a sacred cord. We are true brothers and sisters of the animals".

The second component of the trip was what got me really excited, as it was a chance to live out in the

Kalahari with the Khoisan Bushmen! I had never forgotten the sperm whale's message and I'd longed to somehow record both the whale sound and the Bushmen's ancient language. It had felt so important that I somehow link the energies together, so that I wouldn't fail the whale, who had been so generous with his wisdom for us.

After a gruelling road trip, we arrived at our Kalahari camp and were greeted by these ancient, beautiful, fine boned people, who had the biggest grins and the most infectious laughter! We arrived as a group of 13 women, a number that was said to be most auspicious!

There hadn't been any rain in the desert for over two years, but somehow we managed to change that! Our first evening was blessed by the most beautiful sunset with so many vibrant hues of purple, pink and red.

Suddenly flashes and forks of lightening crashed through the sky and we assumed that it would be an electric storm, as there couldn't be any rain right? A huge wind whipped up and then a deluge of torrential rain thundered down, flooding our tents and most of their contents. I remember lying in my tent feeling around to see how much water was seeping in and I felt it was a little damp, but my tent mate was splashing around in our very own indoor pool. During our three nights that we were there, every night we battled against howling wind and driving rain, grimly hanging onto our tents as they collapsed and were in danger of blowing away, only to meet the dawn with glorious sunshine and clear blue skies. The Bushmen were ecstatic and commended us on our rain making skills!

They said we were very powerful women to bring the rains! The desert seemed to come to life with beautiful flowers and there were so many tell-tale sandy, animal tracks around our camp.

What weren't quite so beautiful, but were quite magnificent, were some of the crawling beings that emerged from their dehydrated sandy homes. Huge giant black millipede like creatures called rain worms, erupted out of the ground everywhere. They were about six to nine inches long and about an inch wide. They were said to be venomous if they crawled on your skin, so I sent them lots of loving respect, but was careful to make sure that I didn't end up sleeping with any in our tent or inadvertently step on them during any trips outside at night!

However I hadn't forgotten my mission to connect with the Bushmen's ancestral wisdom and to hear and record their voice. I spent time with one of the most beautiful souls I had ever met. A San Shaman and medicine man called Izak. He and his wife Lys, pronounced 'Lace', were the tribe's healers and wisdom keepers. I can honestly say that meeting with Izak has been life changing and I'm excited to see how our connection continues to grow, as I can feel his energy every time I send out the intention to connect with him. We sat together holding hands, as I felt the energy move between us. His gnarled, but healing hands, felt so powerful with his firm grip and I had to maintain eye contact looking deep into his soul, as he scrutinised my energy, gazing deep into mine. I felt a blackness circulating between us, but it soon turned into a beautiful glowing, gold, that then seemed to combine us as one immense gold being. I felt that he had transmuted any dark, negative fears and sadness within me, into gold healing energy. He told me that his San name meant Porcupine and he always carried a small bunch of their quills when he was healing. When I gazed into his eyes, all I could see were the eyes of a lion. He told me that I had to look into the eyes of a lion to reclaim my power, and that he would send me a lion to give me this gift. I hadn't told him then about the next part of my South African adventure, which was to return to the home of the sacred white lions!

It was so surreal sitting in the middle of the Kalahari Desert, discussing sperm whale messages! Izak's environment was far from the ocean, but he was totally in tune with the ancient memories of the whale beings and their connections to Atlantis and Lemuria. He kindly allowed me to record his voice, speaking their language and it was so wonderful to hear the 'clicks'.

When writing their words the click is written as an ! Which I think is lovely!

We had a wonderful ceremony with three San Grand-mothers in a sacred site of ancient cave dwellings. One special cave had been, up until recently, inhabited for many years by a Grandmother whose name was Nas. Sadly she had now died, taking with her the last remnants of an ancient way of living. The cave was now inhabited by a large population of rain worms, who we gently coaxed to move out of our way, so that we could all sit in the cave to perform a healing ceremony with the wise women of the tribe. We lit candles in honour of the ancestors, who we felt graced us with their presence and protection. We asked for guidance and healing for humankind to work in harmony with each other and the nature kingdoms to be as one. Later that night in my soggy tent, dodging the drips, I felt her come through to me, as she gave me these words that summed up our ceremony and the honouring of all living beings on mother earth.

The Grandmother Cave

My spirit still rests in this place,
If you look carefully, you will see my face,
I am in the rain worms and insects that crawl,
I am in the rock and the earth and the ALL,
I am in the sun and the moon and the trees,
I am in you and I am in me.

Leaving Izak and the intoxicating expanse of the Kalahari, was so hard, in fact if we hadn't had to journey to our final component of the trip, which was to meet the white lions once more, I don't think I could  have dragged myself away from such beautiful people, who were so loving and generous with their time and healing wisdom. These people have been hunted down and persecuted by white people almost to extinction. They had their land stolen and ravaged and their way of life vilified. Finally the government has allowed some land to be reallocated to them, so that they can maintain their deep connections with nature, as the first hunter gatherers through eons of time. They have so much knowledge about the healing plants and survival skills, which we really need to learn from them. We need to now honour and respect their wisdom and allow them to show *us* how to find our way home! It was so emotional leaving Izak and the rest of the tribe, who had looked after us so well. Writing these words now makes the tears flow in gratitude for their loving guidance that I feel so honoured to share with you. I hope that by reading them, you will feel the Shaman's healing love. I included a photograph of his incredible face; with his lion eyes shining out so that you too fill feel his healing love!

The winds of the Kalahari blow through my soul, clearing the dark dust, Sweeping the cobwebs of doubt, illuminating, like the full moon and the new day's sun's rays. The tiny small boned people share their wisdom and love, empowering and imbuing their ancestral knowledge with gentle humour, blessing us with their care.

As a parting gift, Izak gave me his porcupine quills to use in my healing practice with my clients back in the UK. They nestle on my healing altar as a daily reminder of the beautiful being who has a place in my heart forever.

A return to the White Lion star beings

In her book, *The Mystery of the White Lions… children of the Sun God*, Linda Tucker wrote about the prophesies of the indigenous African people, who believe that when the white lions return to roar in their wild prides, South Africa and the rest of the world can begin to heal. She set out to restore the white lions to their sacred lands in Timbavati and managed to get funding to buy land to create a safe reserve for them, to live in protected harmony once more. I had been sent an email with information about the lions and a photograph of the pride's patriarch, whose energy nearly blew me off my chair, as his ice blue eyes shone out of my computer screen! I knew that one day I would get to meet him! It took me two years but I finally got there.

This was nearly four years ago now, and on the day I had left, I had promised myself that I would return. I wrote about my experiences with the lions in my book *The Whale Whisperer*, but I knew there was much more I had to learn from them. The great white male lion, Mandla, had been the driving force behind by passion and mission to share the wisdom of the animal kingdom and its importance to the future of humankind. On my last visit he had told me

110

"You humans must be lionhearted in your endeavours and step up to the plate to work with the animal kingdom, so that you can work with us to help you help our planet". A young lioness called Nebu was also a very important being, who was going to be instrumental in anchoring the energies for 2012 and the new planetary paradigms beyond. My last encounter with the lions then, had seen Nebu lying next to us, near our jeep, away from her mother and siblings and I communicated with her about the importance of her role in planetary healing work. She seemed to be happy to take on this vital role and I had always maintained extreme interest in her progress, over time, as she matured into a fully grown lioness and couldn't wait to meet her again, now she was in her full power. I had hoped to take a group of people to visit and learn from the lions, but it hadn't quite unfolded in that way, and two years before my return, I channelled some words from an ancient lion being, who called herself Grandmother Leolani, who said she was the matriarch of all lions! This is what she said…

'I fire the constellations and liaise with the moon that connects with the tidal forces, which in turn energises the oceans as the vibrations are translated and assimilated by the whale being consciousness. I am the bridge from the stars to the physical and I oversee all leonine transmuting (and all felines of all cat families large and small). I am queen of the stars and I am senior to Tefnut. Your journey now will be one of giant steps and leaps of faith, of which you will always be rewarded from now on - the time of struggle has long passed. Your road now will be smoothed by the will and protection of the universal laws, now that you have learnt to journey with the flow instead of against it! All is empowerment and enrichment - there is still much to learn, but all is revealed in manageable sections. You will travel to Tsau (the home of the lions) but not with the group that you thought. It will be a personal pilgrimage and not about being paid monetary wise, though you will gain far more than mere money! You will again be a bridge for the bridge. Due to some

frenetic energies, Nebu is not connecting up all the signs. With your physical arrival, this can take place. Mandla awaits your arrival and takes great pleasure in being the driving force behind your endeavours - there is yet far more to come!'

I had written this down in a journal and had forgotten about her words until two years later. I took that journal with me on this trip, and re-read what she had said. It was indeed a personal pilgrimage and everything she had conveyed, made sense on my arrival back at the sacred land of the lions. I was also interested in her connections between the lions and whale planetary work. I had felt that the whale nations and the white lions were working together as co-guardians of the land and the sea, but this trip deepened the message for me even more!

Our first encounter was in the last dying embers of light, I saw Nebu stretched out asleep under the stars, with a full belly with her brothers, after making a kill for them. She had become a fierce huntress and a huge force to be reckoned with. It was so wonderful seeing her again after all that time. She started to send messages into my mind about five pathways within the land that had some blocked energies, which were preventing her from balancing and transmuting some dark energy within the turmoil and trauma of South Africa and the whole African nation. Credo had talked about the atrocities of Apartheid and there was an abominable trade in poaching, bush meat and lions, being bred for trophy hunting. Nebu wanted to work to transmute the very dense vibrations of these, but was being prevented by the blockages. She asked me to ask the group to work with her. I asked Linda if she could identify where these five paths met, rather like a star somewhere on the land. Nebu wanted us to send gold energy through the land also Nebu said there was a huge seam of quartz crystal somewhere in the area and the gold energy would be reflected and refracted, expanding, energising, empowering and recharging, in fact super charging the healing energy throughout the land! Linda managed to locate the area that Nebu was telling me about, so as a group we all visualised sending the gold energy. We all felt that something was clearing and prayed that we had been effective in assisting Nebu's work.

The next morning we met the two fully grown males Regeus and Letaba, who had their own pride with two golden lionesses. As we sat transfixed, watching them playfully roll and tumble about showing such love for each other, Letaba suddenly jumped up and came straight towards me. This huge beast was only a few feet away from our open jeep. He stared right at me and seemed to pierce my soul. His ice blue eyes bored into me, just enough for Izak's words to flood back into my mind *"You must look into the eyes of a lion!"* I then dropped my eyes in reverence, but sent out a huge wave of gratitude from my heart, as I felt the full effect of his immense energy penetrate my whole body, being in such close proximity of such a huge creature!

I was so happy that Letaba had given me the gift of his gaze and I hoped that I was empowered enough to continue my work for the animals. Meeting the magnificent Mandla was always going to be emotional, as he'd had such a profound effect on me, both from a distance and physically. He was now a very old lion and his beautiful mane was now thinning. His hugely powerful limbs were still strong and his massive paws, strode purposefully over his territory. He was a truly awesome being, just being in his presence filled me with love for him. We found him washing his beloved lion wife Zihra's face, with such affection and adoration. We were all deeply moved by his demonstration of love for her. He was showing us the physical concept of un-conditional love that we must have for ourselves and one another. In his display, were all the messages that we needed to learn about love and love conquers ALL!

Then he said to me; *"the lion heart needs to expand and join the divine energy of the blue whale - feel the source of love in my heart and place it in the heart of the blue whale mother, so she can spread it further and heal the earth matrix, combining our forces. THIS IS MY LEGACY... UNITY!"*

I visualised his beautiful heart energy being combined with the memory I had of the blue whale mother's heart, and hoped that I had helped to fulfil my duty to him and to the healing of Mother Earth. It had been my mission ever since our first meeting four years before. I was so sad leaving him the last time, as I wasn't sure that I would ever see him alive again, but I know that I will always be able to seek his guidance and help to be 'lion hearted' to complete my task of sharing his wisdom with humanity.

Since this wisdom was shared, Mandla did indeed pass into spirit in great peace. Three days after hearing about his passing, he came to me at night and showed himself as a beautiful winged lion, soaring through the multiverse, effortlessly cruising the galaxies and dropping in to the earthly planes, whenever he needs to fine tune us even more!

When I visited the sacred site of Amaru Muru in Peru, he came sweeping into me, causing me to emit tremendous roars that I had to give voice to, as I thought if I didn't I would explode! It is a place of huge galactic portals and he wanted me to bring in the star lion energies into that sacred place. The rest of my group looked on, amazed, as the huge roars came out of me, echoing around the valley. I'm not sure what the people living there thought, as the immense sound reverberated around the rocks of the vast valley and bounced off the portal walls. Mandla continues to make his presence felt at some very unexpected times!

Adam's Calendar

During my first visit to meet Mandla in 2009, we were also taken to the incredible escarpment in the Drakensberg

Mountains at a place called Kaapsehoop. There is the most ancient man-made stone circle there called Adam's Calendar. Michael Tellinger has done much research on the origins of this circle and the land surrounding it. In my book "The Whale Whisperer", I wrote about the sacred wild horse herds roaming there, guardians of the unicorn portals. Mandla told me that these horses carried the genetic imprint of the golden Atlantean horses.

The energies in the centre of the two central stones of the circle are phenomenal. The lichen on the outside of one of the huge central stones is formed in the shape of a rampant white unicorn, which you can just see in this photograph.

Of course the energies of the stones are not restricted to just the circle – the whole area is a power house of energy. Many stones, if 'sounded' by banging the surface with a smaller stone, have the most beautiful resonance and have a gong like sound. This is a message I received after spending time with the horses and the stones;

The silent stones lay dormant through eons of time, waiting to be re-awakened. To sing again, to ring again, as their sound resonates down into the earth and up into the cosmos, unifying both worlds and reconnecting the stone structures throughout the land that reach far and wide. Each stone activates the next as the vast mycelium of energy builds and reconnects, recharges, unifying both worlds and reconnecting the stone structures that reach far and wide. Each stone activates the next, as energy builds and reconnects, recharges vibrates it's signals to the beings that laid them there. The web of stones reaches out like outstretched hands, welcoming the new era of awareness. Tapping out their message to the universe, they speak once more, reprogramming the repressed and enslaved, reminding us of our power and self-will and reclaiming our star heritage to re-discover the techniques of harnessing the sound to weave the web, as crystalline structures reunite and repair the grid. The sound vibrates and connects to all the grids and stone/ crystal structures of Mother Earth, where implants from the star beings are positioned.

The domesticated horses that are ridden around the escarpment also run free at night with the wild horses. I was further told that they act as go-betweens with the wild horses, who anchor and spread the stone's energies around the whole area. They carry them in their hooves and energy fields - also connecting to the humans they interact with, bringing the multi-dimensional energies to them. If you feel drawn to explore this area on these wonderful horses, there is a link in the resource section at the back of the book.

The dragon energies are coming through so strongly now forming wonderful healing alliances with many of us. Being in the 'dragon' mountains, on my most recent trip to the stone circle, I was compelled to create a ceremony to reactivate the dragons, I also felt were somehow within the stones. My friend and I had also recently attended a world dragon day at Avebury stone circle in the UK, activating the dragon stones there. The next day we had visited Stanton Drew stone circle to make the connections with the stones there. Whilst there, I felt that we also had to perform a dragon ceremony at Adam's Calendar, which we were due to visit shortly afterwards.

So to celebrate the 'super moon' occurring that evening, back in South Africa, we stood in-between the central stones, in thick low cloud and pouring rain, calling in the dragons. It was the most beautiful, if very damp, experience! There is also a beautiful dragon meditation gifted to you in chapter 10. We were also introduced to a new dragon, who said he was the balancer of rainfall. The surrounding area of Kaapsehoop and the Kruger National Park, had suffered a terrible drought, so we were so pleased to see the rain, even though we were soaked through! We were also relieved in a way that low cloud prevented the super moon to shine through, as on these moonlit nights, many animals in the park would be at risk from poaching, so although we were disappointed not to see the special moon, we were glad that the animals would be safer!

Activating the lions

Also on that recent trip, we were told that we would have the chance to meet some new white lions, kept on a reserve, not too far away from Mandla's former home in Timbavati. When we had seen a photograph of these four lions, I felt Mandla coming in so strongly and he said we had to listen to these lions and reactivate them, reminding them of their star heritage, as they had felt that they had to shut down their connection in order to cope with their captivity. We had several dreams about the lions before our visit. One of the males, we later knew as Eddie, came through asking us to help him, and the night before we met them physically, I dreamt of the two lionesses walking either side of me, purring and protecting me. It was a beautiful dream and I couldn't wait to spend time with them and of course asked Mandla to assist in their reawakening when we were with them.

It was extremely emotional meeting them and feeling Mandla coming energetically, into our midst, guiding us to help these beautiful beings. There were two lionesses Mweti and Nessie, and two males Eddie, as I mentioned and Ringon the dominant male. We were provided with shade and chairs in order to spend time communicating with the beautiful lions, so we sat patiently sending them our love and wondered what they might have to share with us.

The beautiful lioness Marah, who was mother to Zirah, Mandla's mate, came through from spirit gifting Mandla with this message which he conveyed to me;

Marah shines down her starbursts, reactivating their star frequencies, their memory of which has been lost or diminished through the tides of time and space. So many of the children of the sun god have suffered and died because of not being recognised for who and what they truly are. Their lost heritage can be rediscovered and reclaimed. This travesty must be addressed and the reconnection made. The white light that pours from their being can be directly aligned deep into the earth crystal, wrapping around it and through it. This awakens the golden earth energies and rays, co-creating with the cosmic whales... all is good ... all is one! Let the starlight shine from these beings now. Remind them of their magnificence and power to transform and transmute - even behind their bars and wire - they can now journey through the multiverse, with the other guardians. Mandla flies to welcome them!!

I was reminded of the words to the Joni Mitchell song about being golden stardust and returning to the 'garden'. I understood, from Mandla that this meant that humans also had to remember their star heritage and to reconnect with the earth at this vital time.

Marah went on to say;
"There is a great necessity to lift the veils of greed and hatred, melt the hard, harsh heart of humankind, facilitating oneness. Eddie is the

many people on my return, gifting many healing meditations for re-empowerment and continues to do his work prophesied by Mandla.

However on my last visit to the lions, Mweti also had to have her say;

"I am the golden one, you have now reconnected me to the starlight that I had lost. As you say our mission is to shine our light out from and into the earth. Although we are white, we transmit the golden ray, which connects and of course aligns with the golden ray consciousness vibration and frequencies of the cosmic light whales and the 2.9 megahertz. This is now a symbiotic coming together of these mega beings - all is now reactivated with the sacred star energies. Whales, dragons, unicorns, white lions, all unite in perfect unison. The Merkabah co-created, connects us all to the diamond light".

This Merkabah seems to create a diamond like structure thus;

Dragon...   Sky Stars (at the top)
Lions...   Earth Dwellers (in the centre)
Whales...   Libraries of Knowledge of the Inner Earth dimensions (at the bottom)

On that last visit to the lions, I was greeted by the lionesses rushing to their fence and I heard them sending lovely purring greetings to me, which was such a blessing for me, as they seemed to recognise me, rubbing along the fence, wittering their lovely welcome. It's so lovely to be able to still be in touch with them, even back in the cold

UK!

My dear friend Charlotte had also got to know the lions and after her return to her home in the Netherlands, she discovered that there were three white lions in a zoo there and Mandla came through and asked us if we could also activate these sad creatures although I was not able to journey to the Netherlands physically at that time, I knew that I could be with my friends in spirit and the night after their visit, Mandla wanted them to be given their wild Zulu names to reconnect with their true heritage. I asked Mandla what their names should be - Eddie wanted to be called Aslan from then on. So in my half asleep hypnagogic state, I asked to be given their names. Charlotte had told me that one lioness was very reserved and quiet, whilst the other seemed very playful. Sadly the male didn't put in an appearance, but they had definitely felt his presence, as I know he had felt theirs. So the name I was given for the quiet lioness was Silence, which is Atule in Zulu. The playful lioness was to be called Precious and this is Ngabile in Zulu. However the male lion already had his Zulu name, which was Matumba, which means Big Drums!!

I loved the meaning of Matumba - he was shouting at me all night - "THIS IS MY NAME"!!!!! He is sending out his big drums to communicate with us and the stars now!!! I hoped that Mandla was pleased with our work, reconnecting these incredible beings with their wild star-lion pride.

Chapter 8

Water Wisdom

Water is everything! It is a super conductor and each molecule has a whole city of intelligence within it! We have barely scratched the surface of understanding how important water is to us and our planet. It is totally programmable and the potential for its healing powers is immeasurable.

Unchartered Waters

The wonderful male lion Mandla told me to *"find the source"*.

He followed by saying;

"Water shapes everything it is the common denominator in ALL things. The intelligence and knowledge of our loving life giving water is deep inside of you - sail your own waters - journey where no one else has gone, 'here be dragons'! Bring my love source deep inside of you and it will help you go within. Map your own waters that feed your force. Your thoughts feed your water's mind-set, as it circulates your body with the oxygen in your blood. The water memory 'retains' your thoughts in its own cellular brain. Of course this is what causes dis-ease and imbalance in your bodies - your water hears your messages to your self - DIVE DEEP! Water connects us to the ALL - it holds the memory of time and space - the past great civilisations all used water - it still holds the memories and ancient knowledge of those times and how it was used."

He also reminded me of Brock's messages about Orgone. He said that the sound frequencies of cetaceans, deeply affect the water molecules. They transmit Orgone within their sound that is 'downloaded' into the cell memories of water, and can be used to heal all life. Brock said that Orgone energy was the purest form of love and I feel that this is what the whales meant by saying that they imbue every water molecule with their love. Their sound also affects the lunar and tide movement. The 'divine breath' of the blue whales, helps to oxygenate the planet's oceans in conjunction with the trees.

The whales have 'told' me that their sound works on the crystal structures in our skeletal structures and that with our DNA is rapidly changing now, with their healing, our bones can become more crystalline and more in tune with the inner crystalline structures of the planet - connecting us to the planet's vibration.

I was given a very strange vision of being in my mermaid body, where any bone structure was made of crystal and that it was far less dense than normal bone tissue. I saw a huge whale coming towards me. It felt like the white whale mother and she opened her mouth and took me inside her mouth cavity, where she gently held me. Her sound vibrations further fine-tuned my body, creating perfect health by vibrating my cells and their water content, aligning and strengthening me. I was shown that there was a mermaid culture and source of wisdom, which is also stored within our water memory. The whale told me that we can all access this and be healed by the whale sound. I could feel the Orgonic frequencies reshaping and balancing my cell vibration. I saw other mer-beings, also turning more and more crystalline and when they died, it was like their skeletons were super conductors of the healing energy. They showed me the water molecules being full of data - I was shown them tremendously magnified, showing all the symbols and formulae, all contained within the molecules, as the whale's sound fine-tuned literally, and programmed each molecule for whatever healing was required. I thought this was very interesting, as I could 'see' all the information stored, with the water absorbing the technologies 'downloaded' by the whale's vibrations.

where I knew there would be this kind of trap door, but it was small and circular and when I opened it up. I could see very deep dark water below. I knew that I had to squeeze through the narrow opening and go down beneath the water. This filled me with so much fear that it woke me up! However I knew that I had to do this, so I forced myself to visualise being back at the hole and then called in my mer-being body, and then had the courage to descend into the dark water. I found that there was a kind of guide rope that I could hold onto, as I descended. The big breath that I'd taken just before being swallowed up by the dark cold water, seemed to be allowing me to keep going down. Eventually I came to the end of the rope and the bottom of the watery depth. I found a gold treasure chest that was quite heavy, but I knew I had to bring it to the surface. I knew it contained vital information that had to be shared. I swam back up clutching the chest to my heart centre, pulling myself up the rope with my other hand and then bobbed to the surface and slithered back through the hole into the basement.

During our morning dream circle in the Kalahari, Izak translated our dreams, and he was very interested in mine. He said he felt that I had delved into the depths of myself, which had been very scary, as I'd had to trust that I was safe to go in deep into the dark crevices of my memory, to access this knowledge. He said I would write about it and it would be accepted and used to help people heal. I can see how all the components are coming together, I believe this is what heals people who spend time with dolphins, even if their sounds that they use aren't audible to us, their energy vibrations alter the human body, that may be out of balance emotionally or physically, because it affects the water content of their body, harmonising it once more. I feel sure that this also connects with the Orgone healing energy and that everything is connected.

70% of our planet is covered in water, the salt content has

been said to be the same as in our blood. Adults are said to have 60% water content in their body. The brain and heart are composed of 73% water, and the lungs are about 83% water. The skin contains 64% water, and even the bones are watery: 31%. Water helps digest our food so it can provide us with energy, it helps to transport waste out of the body, and it is important in controlling body temperature. The gift of water is everything…

The gift of water is everything…

A year after Brock's first 'downloads', I was rudely awakened once more by the being I recognized as Brock – but this time he gave me some even more surprising information! He reminded me of his Pleiadian origins, but then told me that this was a future incarnation of myself, and that I had come back to help me remember more of my innate wisdom!

This is what I was told:

"The healing frequency of 2.9 megahertz is the healing vibration for the molecular water structures in our bodies - It breaks down the diatoms to create balance and health allowing the Orgone in the atmosphere to restructure healthy, healing cells. Using the encoder click streams and sounds of the whales channeled into the body, creates this transformation of energy toxins in our systems, created by our thought patterns and toxic environments and chemical ingestion through food/water/household products/ pollution etc... However we have far more resistance to all these things if the molecular structure of our cells (water) i.e. the water that is our life support to our cells, is resonating at the right frequency. Sonar can be adapted to utilize the whale's sound frequency 'clicks' to create this frequency and so people can be treated to heal their 'water'!

The water that they drink can also be treated, so that they are ingesting the antitoxins to help clear their systems. In this way the cetacean world can fulfil their role and we as their humble patients can revere and protect them! There will be machines/tools to achieve this - I will guide you to speak to the right people who can build this. This is your medicine thank you for letting me advise you" EB32H.

This was the 'name' he told me I could recognize him by – he said that they do not have names as such just an energy recognition, but he said this was a sector number!

...... I have since been in contact with my 'future' self and been guided with more information. In the future meetings I was to experience such powerful encounters with some incredible whale beings, one of which was Nazkaa, who also guided me as to how to channel and transmit the 2.9 megahertz frequencies, combining her frequencies and integrating the vibration of my future self. More of this in the next chapter!

Chapter 9

The Return of Nagwal and the
Healing Whales of Tonga

I was lucky enough to visit the island of Vava'u off the mainland of Tonga in 2014. We had many incredible encounters with the awesome humpbacks that came into those waters to calve and to breed. There were so many heart centred experiences, but these are the ones that will stay in my heart forever and their loving wisdom and teachings, can now be shared with you!

Convectors and Conductors

Whilst journeying from Tonga to Vava'u, I was gifted a vision of an avenue of golden rods, pillar like formations, being placed in the ocean between the islands. The whales were connecting up these rods and anchoring them into the oceanic grid lines. I was told that upon arrival in Vava'u, the rods would be activated by the whale frequencies and then we would be transmitters to assist with this integration of vibrations, which we are part of. I felt this was preparation for the golden diamond light codes that we were to learn about later.

Nagwal first came to me in a recording session in Glastonbury. He showed himself as an enormous pre-historic whale creature, one of the biggest of the ancient sea creatures, ever to have swum in our oceans. He gifted me the beautiful "Lagoon of Nagwal" meditation, which I shared on the CD "Whale Whispers, Lion Roars". Incidentally Mandla also came into the recording studio to give us his "Lion heart" meditation, so as you can imagine the room became extremely full, with these huge beings, dropping in to share their messages! The wonderful Jerome O'Connell recorded the whale transmission through me and then composed the sound track to accompany the meditation. He played his cello in a way he had never done before, as whale sounds emanated from the instrument. We both became so emotional, as the overwhelmingly beautiful sounds reverberated around the studio. Fat tear drops fell from his eyes onto the cello, as they also ran down my cheeks, in sheer awe of the occasion. I shall never forget the power of that moment, as we wept at the magnitude of the loving message that Nagwal shared with us, as his ancient energy filled the room.

I had always wondered whether Nagwal might ever choose to reincarnate into a physical frequency one day and as we encountered a beautiful courting humpback

couple in the cerulean waters of Vava'u, I was to get my answer! It was the 9th of September 2014 and the night was to be the full moon, called the golden moon.

We floated in the ocean, holding hands, above these enormous whales, as they performed their valentine's dance of courtship. The female I later learnt, was called

Nazia. She was almost white with only a few darker grey patches along her sides and fins. The smaller darker male, cradled her at one point, within his pectoral fins in a loving embrace. They rolled over to show us their hearts. They then dove down into the ocean depths to mate and as we returned to our boat, once more on deck, the couple then exploded, in fountains of ocean froth, in a gargantuan display of leaping, breaching in celebration of their union. The crashing crescendo of sound as they cascaded back into the surface of the sea left us awestruck in wonder. As I sat, still in a state of amazement at what we had just witnessed, I was told that these were to be Nagwal's parents and that we had just been party to his conception. This new golden whale avatar was being created, to bring forth the new golden diamond light codes for the new paradigm of ascension.

I was told we were allowed to be a part of this as I had a vision of a great mothership of lights on the surface of the ocean floor. All the golden rods that I had been shown before were descending into the lights. In my visualisation, I could float down through a golden pillar, down to the ocean floor, anchoring in the columns of light into the grid. It seemed to create a constellation of inverted light galaxies on the floor.

The golden light streamed down to the earth central crystal, turning it gold. Then it radiated the gold light upwards and out of the earth's surface so that the whole earth was shining gold! Because the whales called us to assist in this anchoring of the golden light, they allowed us all to share in the conception of new life - the return of Nagwal! He said the golden full moon was the optimum time for him to be conceived and was of course orchestrated by him for us to assist and bear witness to. Yet another encounter engraved on my heart forever!

A very playful calf

Another encounter with a young calf was a far more light-hearted affair with a young calf learning how to control her body, namely her tail, as she frolicked and thrashed around us. Even though she was young, she still weighed several tons, so the prospect of her breaching and landing on us was still a little dangerous.

However, it was so beautiful to share her exuberance as she swam around us, eyeballing and curiously examining these strange black wet suited blobs in her ocean, with her big knobbly rostrum and piercing, penetrating gaze! We all enjoyed the sheer delight of seeing a free whale in such a beautiful ocean and only when her mother surfaced and decided to move her baby away, did we reluctantly climb back aboard our boat still laughing at the calf's antics.

Whale tears

Every time we set out on the boat, early in the morning, we would stop for a moment and call the whales in, sending them our love and gratitude for whatever encounter we might be blessed with that day. I was asked to lead a little meditation for us all to join hands to participate - even our lovely Captain Andrew and his crew guide Isi joined in. I was given the vision of a beautiful whale crying golden tears, releasing pain and grief from the whaling that had previously been a part of the island's heritage. The knowledge of whale sighting in now fortunately used for whale tourism. Even this has become far too commercialised and the whales are being affected, because of the numbers now infringing on their domain and breeding and calving grounds. So many golden tears flowed from the whale's eye. As tears rolled down my face from the emotion of this vision, the golden tears ceased and then wonderful pink tears started to fall and pink orbs seemed to emanate from every pore of her body, sending out loving forgiveness to the world and humankind. It was such a powerfully emotional vision, which affected our entire group and further showed us the whales' capacity to send love and forgive humankind's ignorance and cruelty. We were later to be blessed with another wonderful encounter that day…

Meeting Nazkaa

Another encounter, this time with a mother whale, was also to change my life and make connections that would assist me in my future healing work.

I had been feeling very sea sick for some reason that day on the ocean. I realise now that it was in preparation for some very powerful energy downloads waiting to be gifted to me, reactivating aspects of my soul DNA, just waiting to be awakened! The only time that the nausea abated, was when I was once more back in the water snorkelling near a beautiful whale mother and her calf. We floated and bobbed about in the rise and fall of the sea for what seemed like ages, as the great whale mother just seemed to float in suspended time, resting as her calf floated alongside her, only surfacing to breathe every five or six minutes. It seemed as though she was holding the space for all mothers. She reminded me of my own mother's love and that of mine for my own children, in a very emotional moment.

Suddenly she seemed to awaken from her trance like stupor and we thought she was about to swim away, when she turned and came right towards us, which was a little disconcerting, due to her immense size!

However she stopped a few feet away from us, and I felt her close inspection of us, as though she was scanning and balancing all our energy and chakra systems in our bodies. The penetrating gaze of her beautiful eye seemed to bore into my very soul. I then got the sense that she was emitting filaments of coloured light, blue, pink, silver and gold. I could really feel her loving healing energy, penetrating deep within me. Then, just as suddenly, she swam away, disappearing into the vastness of the ocean with her young calf. However this was to be just the start of her relationship with me, as she has since come through to me many times, teaching me more about our encounter and what it would enable me to do with the energy downloads she gifted me… a blessed encounter indeed.

Upon my return to the UK, she appeared with such force in a vision, which helped me to understand the role she was to play in assisting me with my healing techniques. Many of which had been taught to me by the animal kingdom both large and small! She told me that the filaments of light she had sent out were activating my ability to transmit the 2.9 megahertz divine feminine frequencies that my future Pleiadian self, had told me about. The first technique she shared with me was to imagine people or animals wrapped within a beautiful Merkabah, gently rotating and together we could transmit the special frequency into the person or animal, cleansing them of anything that no longer served them, either physically or emotionally. When using this technique with groups, Nazkaa suggested that I invite people to have some water near them, so that she could also activate and imbue the water molecules with this healing frequency. This could be drunk afterwards; retaining some to activate more water and also to be used in the cleansing of water sources e.g. lakes, streams, rivers and the sea.

She also showed me a beautiful visualisation where people could restore and heal their past, present and future DNA. The meditation containing this healing technique can be found in chapter 10 towards the end of the book. That night after meeting Nazkaa, I felt my future self come through to me, saying;

"The oceanic trident is perpendicular to the star nebulae from the light beams between Sirius and the Pleiadian collective in conjunction with the star galactic matrix. The mediation points correspond to the Southern Cross Medulla, which is connected to the heart of the cosmos. This connects with the medulla of the planetary and solar systems".

It was one of those moments when I felt I understood what the meaning of this was, but upon waking the next morning, the understanding of this seemed to evade me!

Return to Tonga to find Nagwal

The following year, I was lucky enough to return once more to Vava'u in October 2015, to reconnect in the physical with the humpbacks and to see if we could find Nagwal, who would have been birthed earlier in August. I wondered what beautiful beings I might meet in further blessed encounters. However, I was saddened to see so many more boats out chasing the whales, harassing them with captains that had no respect for the delicate balance of the whales' freedom to be allowed to calve and breed in reverence to their needs. Boats full of noisy tourists, leaping into the water, laughing and screeching, frightening the new mothers and terrorising and exhausting new calves. They were also interfering with the heat runs, where the males vie for their mates, in their titanic battles for supremacy. Luckily our Captain always went in the opposite directions to these 'cowboy' outfits, and always waited patiently, assessing whether a mother might be happy with us entering the water with her and her calf.

Lenali

One such female floated nearby. We saw her tiny calf blowing its diminutive spout next to her. Every time we inched a little nearer with our boat, she swam away a little further along the coast line. She could have completely swum away, but instead seemed to keep us waiting, anticipating a possible encounter in the water with her. However, she continued to move her calf away from us, so we decided that she was unhappy with us entering the water in close proximity. So we just stopped the boat and sent her and her calf, love. As we tuned into her, she showed us some of the whales' distress and it was the first time I had really felt the whales despairing of us humans - in fact it made me feel ashamed to be human, as we have caused so much devastation to these beautiful higher dimensional beings. My previous encounters with humpbacks, had always felt as though they only wanted to remind us of love, but this whale was showing us, how far we had strayed from that concept. Once she had gifted us this message, she swam right under our boat, as if to anchor her words into our psyche. Fortunately my friend was able to capture her enormous presence as she glided past, with their go-pro camera, which captured her passing by, demonstrating that it was then time to leave us, as she had delivered her message to us and it was time to take her calf to safety and seclusion. She later told me that her name was Lenali, and that she wanted us to vision healing portals for the whales to enter to receive healing and cleansing of the trauma caused to them by humankind. Her meditation again is included in chapter 10. I was so happy that we at least could do something to rectify or atone for our desecration and disrespect, in some small way. We spent most of our time on this trip, above water sending healing to the whales and the oceans, as it felt far more important than seeking more physical encounters, though a little disappointing, as being eye to eye next to a whale, immersed in their energy is beyond compare. Only on the last couple of days, were we gifted with some incredible encounters where the whales seemed happy to interact with us.

Finding Nagwal

Although we weren't sure if we had physically encountered Nagwal, we certainly felt his energy and again on one of our 'pauses' on the boat to call him in. He gifted me with yet another wonderful meditation to open hearts and he talked about the new golden diamond heart crystals that he wished to share with us, to open the hearts of man to the new golden diamond light rays coming into the earth, to further assist our ascension. His healing meditation is also part of Chapter 10. In the meditation he showed me him touching people with his pectoral fin on their third eye and then their heart, as though opening their whale eye and then gifting the golden diamond light crystal into the hearts of humankind. We were amazed to hear from our captain, that a male calf had been videoed doing just this with someone swimming with him. He had gently touched them on the forehead with the tip of his fin and then their heart centre. He had also been seen fearlessly leading a heat run, unheard of behaviour for a small calf! He had very distinctive markings, easily recognised by our captain, who knew many of the mothers and their calves, having sailed in those waters for many years. So his meditation encapsulates what he showed me in my vision, but also what he performed in physical reality!

Chapter 10

Gifts from the Guardians of Gaia

Meditations from the guardians to heal yourselves and the earth

Tree Wisdom for life purpose and heart reconnection

So making yourself comfortable, feel yourself really connecting, as you sit in your chair, or lie on the floor ... feel the strength and the beauty of Mother Earth beneath you – feel her love supporting you ..... holding you .... and so taking three lovely long deep breaths, noticing the cool air as you breathe in .... and the slightly warmer air as you breathe out .... and with each out breath, allow yourself to relax more and more .... with each out breath, allow yourself to absorb more and more peace .... with each out breath feel your body just letting go .... and when you are ready, imagine that you are standing in the most beautiful beam of light ..... and as you visualise stepping through this beam of light, you find that it becomes rays, shafts, of sunlight ,and you find yourself in the most beautiful meadow, and you are walking on a soft path, and you can feel the warmth of the sun on your face, and a slight breeze in your hair... and you can hear the wild birds all around you and high above you ... the smell of the grass and the fragrance of the wild flowers, pour into you, giving you a sensory overload of joy of the beauty of this place .... of this wonderful place .... and as you walk along the path, ahead of you .... you notice a small copse of trees, and as you draw nearer, one tree in particular, seems to be calling you .... it seems to be drawing you nearer .... this is a very ancient tree, a very wise being and within this tree are all the answers to all your questions, for you are an earth keeper .... and at this momentous time in the planet's history, you have to know more about your healing role in order to best serve Mother Earth. So allow yourself to be drawn closer and closer .... leaning your face against the trunk, inhaling the beautiful sweet fresh aroma of the bark .... feeling with your hands, the velvet of the moss that wraps around the base of this tree .... and the more you connect with this beautiful ancient being, the more you feel a part of it ..... and as if by magic ... part of the trunk opens up, and you are allowed to step inside .... to your amazement it is very light, and you feel very safe, and you can see a long staircase leading downwards ... and you make your way down and down, step by step .... until you find yourself in a corridor, where there are doors leading off, and you feel the need to search for the door that has a sign upon it saying Tree Wisdom .... so make your way along the corridor and find the door ...... and when you find the door, notice the writing, the colours, the textures .... and finding the handle, either turn or push the door open, stepping inside the room of Tree Wisdom .... and once inside, have a really good look around, noticing the contents, how does it make you feel? Inside the room, waiting for you, is the guardian ...... ask the guardian to step forward now, or to make its presence felt, as you humbly ask for advice and help, and what you need to know at this moment in time to help to you on your journey, so that you may be better equipped to help Mother Earth ...... so out of the shadows the guardian appears .... ask all your questions that you wish to know the answer to at this moment in time .... and knowing that you can return at any time to gain more knowledge, and yet more wisdom, but just for now it's time to thank the guardian for all their help .... and before you leave this room, the guardian will show you a small token, a small gift, that holds the energy and the wisdom of this room, that you can take with you, so that you may instantly reconnect whenever you wish .... so feel the gift placed in your hand ...... and thanking the room, the guardian, the energy of this wisdom .... you make your way back to the door, placing the gift in your pocket, and stepping back through the door, closing it gently behind you, and then making your way a little further along the corridor, looking for another door, and you are looking for the   door into the room of Mother Earth .... so making your way along the corridor, and finding the door with the sign that reads Mother Earth ...... again notice the door, is it old? Is it new? Is it just wood? Is it coloured? notice the handle .... and again turning or pushing the handle, open the door, and step inside, closing the door behind you and notice again the contents of this room, the textures. All the details .... and ask the guardian of this room to step forward again, to bring you more information, more knowledge, more tools to help you with your work .... greeting the guardian now thanking them for taking the time to help you, ask how you can help Mother Earth? .... and knowing that information will help you as a servant, as an earth keeper, as a sacred activist .... and thanking the guardian for all their advice ...... knowing you can return again any time, but just for now it's time to leave the room, but there is yet another gift for you .... allow it to be placed in your hand, again this holds the energy, the wisdom, the instant connection ..... the instant reconnection, to this beautiful energy whenever you wish .... and so placing the second gift in your pocket ... making your way back to the door ..... Opening and stepping once again, back out into the corridor, closing it behind you .... you then make your way back towards the stairs, but on your way, there's one last room that you are looking for, and it is the room of love.... for love is all there is .... and so finding the door with the words 'love' written, carved, whatever way you can see it, whatever way you find this door ..... finding the handle and opening the door and stepping inside into the room of love . ... and again drinking in all the details, all the textures, all the colours .... as you gaze around in amazement, and you feel your whole body being filled with love .... and the guardian of the room of love steps forward and shows themselves..... welcoming you ....

emitting so much love ,so much compassion .... wrapping you in that love .... and so ask whatever you need to know about the love that you need in your life – the love you can give others, and the love you can give Mother Earth – let them guide you now .... for we need to learn how to receive and to give .... and thanking the guardian for their love, for their patience .... for all that they have given you ...... and as they place a third and final gift in your hands, you may take their gift of love away with you, to continue helping you to receive more and more love into your life, so that you may be able give more and more love............ And so with huge gratitude, thanking the guardian, knowing that you hold their love deep within you now ..... Deep within your heart.... you can make your way back to the door .... opening the door, closing it behind you, and then making your way back up the stairs .... up and up, step by step .... until you find yourself standing once more in the centre of the trunk..... And again it opens up, and you are allowed to step through, as the trunk seals behind you ...... you turn and stare, knowing that this is a secret between you, and this ancient tree being ..... and thanking the tree, so much for keeping you safe, for holding your wisdom, for being there, for permitting you to enter .... You turn and make you way back along the path ...... back out into the sunshine. Once again, feeling the warmth upon your face and the gentle breeze in your hair ..... the sound of the birds .... the smell of the grass, and the wild flowers .... stepping back into the beam of light .... And finding yourself gently drifting back into your body .... into you room ..... just resting a while absorbing and assimilating all the information, all the wisdom, all the love ... that you have received ...... just taking your time ...... and then very gently bringing yourself back, taking a nice deep breath .... Opening your eyes whenever you are ready.

Conversation with a wise standing being

Wise One Speaks

"Be the voice of love for the animals! Connect all life... connect all with love! Love is all there is. There is nothing else to know. Be at peace with yourself. Like me you have many faces, many facets - let them all be from love especially for yourself. You do not love all facets of yourself and so you don't always feel worthy of all you desire. It is all there for you, just allow it. It will be truly wonderful.

Like me reach up to the stars and they will come down for you. Keep reaching higher, so they can connect with you. If you don't put out your hand they cannot reach it or you!

Feel the interconnectedness with all, as my branches entwine, so I show you how everything can entwine and interact with each other. All is One.... That is all I have to say! In love and peace"

Wise one.

Roots in Atlantis - light crystal activation - dolphin healing

The dolphin dream of joy ..... welcome to our world ... you are here to learn the art of play, you humans come here with your fixed agendas and expectations, more pressure to accumulate ... once you let go and open your heart to joy ... look what happens! We show you the art of joy and play, as our sounds resonate

139

through your body ... we infect you with our joy! Every cell contains the dolphin joy that you sadly lack ... we understand so much through eye to eye contact .... when do you play? When do you truly feel joy? Enjoy the feeling of being in our midst as we dash and frolic around you ... hold the awe and magnitude of joy that we share. We show you the art of being in the joy of the moment ... call this in whenever you are too serious and we will remind you. Life is to be enjoyed and fulfilled ... it is a precious commodity, as is the planet, you are here as caretakers, but we feel it is you who need to be cared for and educated in the art of life and living... and so making yourself comfortable, start by taking three lovely long deep breaths...... all the way in .... and all the way out .... feel that gentle rise of your tummy as you breathe in .... and gentle fall as you breathe out .... imagine yourself in a cloak of light .... protecting you, guiding you, cushioning you... The dolphins speak of joy, they speak of forgiveness, they show us a time in the past from which we still hold guilt within our DNA. Call in their energy now and allow them to guide you back .... back to that time to forgive yourself, to let go of the old energies of pain and guilt, that are still wrapped inside the strands of your DNA within you ...... so again with each out breath, release any tension in your body .... give yourself permission to just be .... and notice with each out breath, how beauty-fully your body responds, by relaxing and releasing more and more .... and so when you are ready, imagine that the soles of your feet can open up, and that you can grow the most beautiful roots down through the floor, down through the earth ..... down and down, deeper and deeper .... past the minerals, past the crystals, down and down, through time .... further and further .... back through time ..... until at last your roots touch down into the most beautiful deep lake ..... you can feel the cool water and it has the most beautiful colour blue that you could ever imagine..... This is an inner lake between worlds and in whatever way feels right for you, allow your core essence, that part of you that seeks to be healed, that part of you that needs to journey back to be cleared.... to gain forgiveness and deep peace *and joy .... so visualise this core essence of yourself travelling down now, through your body, down through your roots... down and down and down ..... knowing you are very safe, very much loved, very protected .... and as you find yourself entering the beautiful lake, there are four huge guardians .... huge beings of light that have a wonderful transparent luminescence ..... These are the guardians of Atlantis and they hold your space. They welcome you and they call the dolphins to come to guide you now .... your*

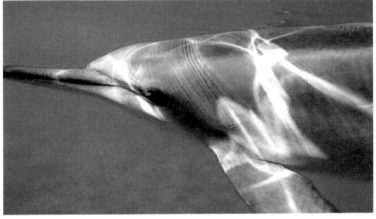

dolphin arrives ... greeting you .... smiling up at you ... beckoning you .... calling you to follow it beneath the surface of the water ... and to your amazement, you are able to be led down into the depths of this lake, breathing easily, travelling effortlessly, drawn along by this beautiful dolphin, that leads you through a short tunnel, that is very light and bright, ... and when you come to the end of the tunnel, you are lifted by the dolphin to the surface, and you step out into the most incredible landscape..... this is the golden age of Atlantis... there are wonderful temples, wonderful scenery all around ... and although your dolphin waits for you can make your way back to your beautiful dolphin friend waiting for you .... and on your way back to the water, you find a tiny piece of light crystal glistening beneath your feet, you ask permission to take back this tiny piece .... this can allow you to connect with the healing and all your ancient wisdom .... and so stepping down into the water, the dolphin leads you back gently, taking you beneath the surface, and once again it feels so safe, so easy to travel through the water, back through the tunnel, back up to the surface .... and you see the four guardians looking down and smiling at you.... they are so happy that you have returned and been freed of the guilt, and being forgiven, we can truly be whole again..... And so thanking your beautiful dolphin .... honouring the Atlantean guardians, thanking them for holding the space .... and knowing that you could return at any time, but just for now it's time to journey back .... so imagine your essence journeying back now, up your roots, up and up, back through time, up and up .... gently re-entering you human body.... taking your time ...... and just drinking some of the Atlantean water up your roots .... it may appear as a blue gold energy .... or blue silver .... see what feels right for you .... breathe up the beautiful Atlantean ancient water energy .... as it fills your being and replenishes your soul .... and then imagine it wrapping you ... wrapping you in joy and love, as you bring up your roots, all the way up into your feet .... and just rest allowing your body to adjust to its new way of being .... as every cell adjusts to the healing that has taken place .... so taking a deep breath allowing your body to move and stretch .... opening your eyes whenever you are ready.

Banishing fear with Archangel Michael - personal and planetary Healing

Finding a soft safe place either sitting or lying down, just allow all thoughts to float away ... being very gentle with yourself ... allow each out breath to drain away any tension ... with each out breath feel yourself going deeper ...... imagine that you are wrapped in the most beautiful, pink shimmering light.... the pink light of love ...... focus your attention on your heart centre ... know that you are so protected, so loved, and as you focus on your heart, imagine your heart to be a beautiful bud and within the bud, lie all the potential and expansion of blossoming and freedom .... and whenever you are ready, imagine with each out breath, that this bud can start to open ... and as each petal unfurls, you feel a release and an expansion ... allow the pink energy of love to flow into you .... you might imagine some kind of cobweb around this beautiful bud, but the more you breathe into it, the more you expand it ... the web dissolves and the petals burst forth .... and this web symbolises just old pain, old hurt, instilled fear within you .... one by one the petals expand, showing the beauty within you ... now you know that it is safe to open your heart to rid yourself of all pain and all fear – see how wonderful that feels .... feel that energy of love fill your whole body from the top of your head to the tips of your toes .... and now focussing on your feet, imagine they can open up, and you can grow the most beautiful roots, down through the earth ... deeper and deeper and deeper .... down .... down and down, and down .... all the way down, until you connect with the core crystal of Mother Earth ....
this immense crystal holds all Gaia's wisdom ... all the planet's memory feel your roots connecting, wrapping around the crystal and then send your love down your body, down the roots .... send your love deep into Mother Earth .... know that you are making a commitment to help her, for the only true power is the power of love, and through love we will conquer all limitation, all fear .... so now that you have made that commitment and sent as much love as you can down into the earth, visualise now drawing up the crystalline energy ... up through

your roots, up and up and up .... into your body ... feel your skeletal structure become as one with the crystal .... becoming as one with the soul memory of Mother Earth ....feel yourself shimmering with crystal energy .... you are now equipped to help Mother Earth, you have the codes, the keys, the transmissions of the memory within you ..... you may now draw your roots back up ..... and up and up and up ..... thanking Mother Earth .... bringing the roots all the way back up into your feet and allow the soles of your feet to seal over once again, sealing in all that beautiful crystal energy within ...... and so now that you are free of fear, full of love, full of power, imagine yourself being lifted up by the most beautiful beings .... beings of light ... lift you up through the sky, through the clouds... higher and higher ...... up into the stars .... and we feel the presence of Archangel Michael ..... we see his sword of truth and its beautiful blue light that shines out. Feel him embody you .... feel him allow you to use the sword of truth .... for as you look down on Mother Earth, as you look down on the planet ... you can see that it is wrapped in this web.... in this web of fear ... and you can see thick cords moving out into the earth's atmosphere ..... And so with Michael's guidance, in whatever way feels right for you .... cut these cords now ... sever these restrictions ..... The web that is incarcerating the planet, free it now! .... and with each cord that you cut, look down on the planet and notice how it responds ..... Notice that it may look lighter .... brighter .... areas of the ocean seem clearer ...... mountains shrouded in mist become clear ...... forests thrive ..... bear witness to this change, this healing, that is taking place .... and give thanks ..... knowing that with Michael's guidance you may revisit this vision of the planet whenever you wish, so that you may perform yet more healing. But just for now it's time to return ... time to come back .... so allow yourself to be gently lowered back.... back down through the stars ..... through the clouds .... down through the sky .... gently back down into your room ..... back into your human physical form .... this physical form that is now transformed into a being of love ... a being of light .... and so just rest a while .... absorbing and assimilating all your experiences .... we give thanks to Michael .... we send our love once more to Mother Earth, and we send love to ourselves .... and so taking a deep breath ... and opening your eyes whenever you are ready.

Finding your Dragon Heart

The story behind this meditation is as follows;

My lovely Dutch friend Charlotte, took a picture of a beautiful orange/red dragon fly in her garden in the Netherlands, who had alighted near her and seemed determined to 'chat' to her! It said that she needed to send me the photo, so that I could 'ask' it to give me a meditation to share. Dutifully, she obeyed the dragon fly

and sent me the photo. About two hours later, another Dutch friend of mine Sunny, who at that time had never met or spoken with Charlotte, also sent me a picture of an orange/red dragon fly, exactly the same kind, with exactly the same message! So of course I had to pay attention to this 'coincidence'! I asked the dragon fly what they would like to share with us, and this is their meditation…

Imagine a beautiful dragon fly before you, beating its iridescent wings….. its illuminated body of translucent colours shines out. Its beauty is so great that it startles you into really noticing this special being that is summoning you to pay attention, as though you have been chosen by this insect, to hear or see what it has to show you. Once you open your mind and heart to its presence and feel its beautiful gentle energy, so that you know that you are safe, to your amazement the dragon fly begins to grow and grow, then metamorphoses into a huge beautiful dragon, who almost seems to smile down on you with gentle eyes, as though so happy to have made this connection with you. Notice does the dragon feel male or female? Notice their colour and form… The dragon comes with gifts of special jewel-like scales under its belly. They shine almost like diamonds and are offered for your highest projected potential - they are offered as portals into the dragon worlds of 7th dimensional realms. This dragon's energy is healing and expansive and allows you to wing your way with them into flights of fancy, but powerful healing for yourself and the universe. They come now at this time RIGHT NOW, as the time is now to once more connect with the beings who have already transcended earthly limitations - they show us that we too can be like this! The unicorns have been showing themselves far more widely now - entering our consciousness more and more. The dragons are coming very carefully, as there has been much fearmongering about them. They are water, air and earth spirits and connect by flying through the portals in between.

Holding your chosen jewelled scale, place it on your heart centre and absorb the jewelled light- it is very gentle, but also very powerful. Feel your body changing into the most beautiful dragon! Suddenly your wings burst out and you practice flapping them and as you do so, your body starts to levitate, as you realise the power you have now to fly between worlds, or over the earth and other planets to receive an overview of their condition or energies. You are able to enter many realms and universes, as the dragons have no barriers to their healing travels. So by connecting with them and being as one with them, you can also enter and give healing where it is needed, using fire and breath to clear darkness and negativity. This fire can be very restorative - it is not about destruction, it is about re-creation and expansion. Journey now wherever the dragons lead you, learning what needs to be healed now.... reconnecting with other beings along the way, maybe meeting master dragons, who can guide you further, maybe they can show you specific dragon gateways or pathways into and on the earth and other realms? Go fly now......... Whenever you are ready, bring back everything you have learnt or been shown. Allow your dragon being self to land and let your wings fold back into your body once more as you gently absorb and assimilate all that you have brought back with you - allowing your body to gently revert to its human form. Imagine your hands still placed on your heart centre, where the jewel scale now resides. By placing your hands on your heart centre with the intention of activating your dragon body once more, you will now be able to journey with them at will! Thank the dragon beings for their gifts and healing love, now bestowed within you and gently bring your awareness back to the room.... Opening your eyes whenever you are ready.

Dragon flight through the multiverse to our alternate earth for profound healing

Once again start by taking three lovely long deep breaths, all the way in and all the way out .... if you feel able, as you exhale allow a sound to emanate from your being in a lovely long Ahhhhhhhhhhh! .... Opening your heart to the limitless possibilities and multi-dimensional potentials that surround you now .... Really feeling your connection to Mother Earth ... Our beautiful Gaia ... feel your feet or your body really connecting with our planet............... breathing as one with her. You feel so much love and allow yourself to connect to your life purpose ... Why you are here right now? Why did you come now? How can you be of service? What do you need to learn? You ask to be guided as to how you can access the wisdom and resources, which you need to fulfil your true potential for your highest good and that of the planet. Know that there is so much guidance and healing available to you now, if you can just open your heart and mind to the possibilities.

So whenever you are ready, imagine that you are standing in the most beautiful forest glade with the trees... the wise ones... the standing people... all around you... It is the time of year where they have shed their leaves, as they start their regeneration through the coming winter season...... you are standing in a carpet of leaves and then suddenly, the leaves begin to swirl and you are aware of this rush of air and you hear the sound of beating wings. As the leaves dance and swirl more and more and the rush of air becomes stronger and stronger and to your amazement, you realise that the dragons are coming .... they are coming through time and space to meet you .... and this magnificent dragon lands gently next to you .... and it seems to smile at you and its wonderful eye fixes you in a loving gaze, but piercing its fire energy into your being. However you feel no fear and in fact feel that the dragon is calling you ... guiding you to answer the urge to climb onto its back, as though it is inviting you ... and so you climb onto its back feeling its scales ... but it feels warm and very safe ...... it gently starts to move its wings, making sure that you are secure and safely positioned, as it starts to rise with its huge wings beating, lifting you up and up through the treetops, up through the sky ... up through the clouds ... higher and higher up into the cosmos and you realise that around you there are thousands of other dragons and it's as though each dragon comes to introduce itself to you ... a beautiful white dragon of purity, Unison, comes and touches wingtips with your dragon, so that the energy of purity and unity flows into your dragon and so into you ... as you feel that you become part of your dragon .... the glorious white energy of Unison pours into you, filling you with the lighter

*light, the lighter light of unity, of unification, of oneness
.... and then when Unison has completed her download
of the lighter light, she flies away... as you continue flying
through the constellations and past the planets... the immense
purple dragon Lanmaark, comes closer to you and he explains to
you that he is a way shower, but he is also a cleanser, sweeping
away negative energies with the vast expanse of his wings, he is
here with his consorts to cleanse the planet – he transmutes the
darkness, the dark fields he sweeps with his wings and
transmutes the dark into the light ... and then many more
dragons come to introduce themselves to you, perhaps your
healing dragons – dragons that you already work with, or the
ones that you will work with in the future......... and you feel
that you are on a mission, that all of you are flying towards
somewhere special .... and you realise, as you begin to
descend slightly... that you are flying towards what looks like
another earth ... and all the stars are twinkling as you wiz by
them, so this is an earth where an alternate you exists but this
you has a different life ...... this life on this planet in this
dimension, you have made different choices, so imagine your
dragon really gently flying into and onto the surface of this other
earth, this alternate universe ..... and in whatever way feels
right for you, imagine descending from your dragon and find
your alternate self............................ and ask them about
their choices, what can you learn from them what can they learn
from you??? Perhaps this alternate earth is an earth of
harmony, of love, of gentleness. Perhaps by connecting with
your alternate self, you can absorb that?? Perhaps if you have
any emotional or physical issues in your body, you can somehow
overlay their energy, which can fill you with health, allow the
loving   frequencies of this planet to be imbued into you ...
so that you may bring it back ... and imbue it into our own
planet, so somehow you can absorb the energy of this beautiful,
beautiful earth and bring it back with you... the dragon brought
you here to show you that this exists... this already exists and
that we can access this ...... so see what this feels like
experiencing the vibration and the frequencies of this planet ...*

of this earth .... and know that you can revisit and bring people and animals into the frequencies of this planet, to meet their alternate selves and that the energy of the alternate selves, can over lay and download health ... healthy cells, healthy emotions... peace and happiness, joy... by being here you can reclaim your joy ... and you can facilitate others in reclaiming their health and their joy their reason for being.. and so thanking your alternate self ... feeling the frequency of this beautiful loving planet ... climb back onto your dragon, who has been waiting patiently for you to experience this and is so happy to have brought you here and then once again finding your balance ... the dragon starts to beat its wings and again lifts you up ... up and up ... up into the stars and again you see all the other legions of dragons flying with you in formation, bringing you back, zooming through the stars so fast ... whizzing into the current earth's atmosphere down and down, through the sky as the clouds fly past you and gradually slowing ... to come to the tree tops beneath you and very softly and gently floating downwards back into the leafy glade once more ... again all the leaves swirl and are tossed about as your dragon lands ... and just rest a few moments with your arms around the dragons neck, resting your head against him... feeling your heartbeat connect with the heartbeat of your dragon ... beating as one... as you thank them for the gift of flight and the gift of knowledge, of healing, of knowing ... that there is so much love and harmony, there is so much peace ... and by connecting with all of that, we can be as one ... as we can overlay the joy, the harmony of that alternate earth onto our earth, transmuting war, poverty, fear ... lack ...... feel the joy of the frequency of our alternate earth envelope and wrap the energy of unity all around our earth .... filling every atom with joy ... every particle ... and once again thank your dragon, slowly climb down standing in the leaves once more - giving your dragon a final hug... and you wonder if you have imagined it, but you are looking at its eye and it seems to give you a wink - a wink of knowing... the knowing that you can call this dragon whenever you wish, to fly through the cosmos, to fly as one, to call in all the other healing dragons... Unison ... Lanmaark ... and any of the dragons that you have connected with, whenever you wish ... but just for now it's time to bring yourself back to the room, being very, very gentle with yourself .... bringing back all the healing, all the love, all the joy .... taking a nice deep breath ... and opening your eyes whenever you are ready.

Connecting with the Olani the Inner Earth beings

I had always felt a strong connection with beings from inside the earth, as well as the outer dimensions. They told me that they were the Olani and this is their meditation for you to journey to meet and learn from them yourself...

Once again finding a soft safe space... making yourself comfortable and gently close your eyes... take three lovely long deep breaths ... all the way in and all the way out - each time you breathe out – allow yourself to sink deeper and deeper into the wonderful being that you already are ... sink deeper and deeper into your place of power and knowing... feel the gentle rise as you breathe in and gentle fall as you breathe out ... allow all chattering thoughts to be banished from your mind – really feel the connection with Mother Earth... Imagine you can feel her breathing beneath you, as you breathe in imagine Mother Earth breathing in, as you breathe out; imagine Mother Earth breathing out ..... imagine your heart beat connecting with the heartbeat of Mother Earth ...so breathing in breathing out .... really feel Mother Earth breathing with you .... and then imagine yourself in the most beautiful meadow ... feel the warmth of the sun on your face and slight breeze in your hair, you can smell the grass .... and feel the soft earth beneath your feet ... hear the birds singing ... and the buzz of the insects ... and you start to walk along this lovely path through the meadow ... and you start to become aware of a presence around you, almost in the corner of your eye, but not quite seeing just feeling and you can imagine perhaps little tinkling laughter and as you continue to walk along, ahead of you are some beautiful trees... and these wise ancient trees are calling you ... calling you and drawing you ever closer ... and as you draw close to the trees you see they are in a circle formation and you feel this ancient presence of the trees ... just know these are huge wise beings ... that have called you here today but it feels as though you have to ask permission to step into the circle, and as you look closely, you see appearing, a golden orb of light that seems to be rising up from inside in the inner earth ... and you realise that inside the orb are these beautiful golden inner earth beings – these are the Olani ... and with their changes of vibrations and frequencies, they allow themselves to be seen, they allow themselves to become physically present, filling the circle and they are smiling at you ... they are inviting you to come into their midst, they wish to converse with you ... they wish to exchange energy with you ... they wish to thank you for your willingness to be of service to our beloved Mother Earth, they know that you care deeply about her ... so perhaps if you feel able, you can sit amongst them... to be held by their presence ... Perhaps you feel able to allow them to guide you deep into Mother Earth, perhaps they can show you aspects of Mother Earth that need healing, and maybe there are things that you need to learn .... so in whatever way feels right for you, allow them to guide you, perhaps you can step through the orb ...... in whatever way feels right, allow them to guide you now deep into our Mother, perhaps in to the inner earth oceans, or lakes, the inner earth realms .... know you are very much loved and very safe – with them now and see where they lead you .... and with your beautiful heart energy that you have, ask the Olani to show you how to give healing to any areas of imbalance that has been shown, imagine shining your light into any of the places that you're being shown that show imbalance, disharmony and humankind's mistreatment of our Mother, the Olani need our help .... and then just by being there bringing the light, you can be of assistance, you can help!...................................... and maybe you can ask the Olani if they can clarify anything you

*need to know about yourself, why are you here? Who are you –
are you a hybrid? What is your role? Why did you come here
what is your purpose?? The Olani know who you are and why
they have invited you to assist them .... and
know that you can visit them any time, you can visit the inner
earth planes anytime you wish to learn more, to give more, to
receive more, to shine your light more, but just for now it's time
to allow them to gently bring you back up into the glade of trees,
up through the golden orb ... finding yourself surrounded by the
beautiful golden Olani, almost in a group hug of energy of
gratitude and love ...... and you feel such an affinity with them
.... and then you feel that you need to just step back ... back
to the trees and then all the Olani gather together creating the
golden orb once more and softly lowers itself down into Mother
Earth and thanking the trees, the ancient ones for holding the
space for this incredible meeting, this incredible journey, that
you've just experienced and then you turn and walk away,
finding your path once more, walking back into the sunlight
through the meadow, feeling the sun, smelling the grass, feeling
the soft earth beneath your feet... until you come to the place
where you started your journey and then just rest a few
moments, absorbing and assimilating everything you
experienced - everything you've learnt – everything you've been
reminded of .... just breathing all that knowing through
your body ...... once again feeling Mother Earth beneath your
feet, but really having a deeper connection to her now .... having
experienced her inner realms, it feels like you know her more,
you understand some of the trauma she has been processing for
us .... you understand that Mother Earth has her own
soul, her own contract as our planet ... that we are all one, we
are all interconnected, we are all on this journey together
.... we are one ...... so the birds are celebrating .... they
are singing, rejoicing in the healing that has taken place ...
perhaps you can sense the Olani celebrating beneath
you! .... and suddenly you are
surrounded by golden butterflies, they flutter and dance all
around you caressing your cheek, landing on you momentarily,*

153

thanking you .... and just as suddenly fly away ...... they just came to give you a divine thank you .... and so very very gently, start to bring your awareness back to the room, take a lovely soft deep breath ... still feeling that inner light ... that you know you can shine wherever it is needed ... and opening your eyes whenever you are ready just taking your time.......
thanking the trees, the ancient ones for holding the space for this incredible meeting, this incredible journey, that you've just experienced and then you turn and walk away, finding your path once more, walking back into the sunlight through the meadow, feeling the sun, smelling the grass, feeling the soft earth beneath your feet... until you come to the place where you started your journey and then just rest a few moments, absorbing and assimilating everything you experienced - everything you've learnt – everything you've been reminded of .... just breathing all that knowing through your body ...... once again feeling Mother Earth beneath your feet, but really having a deeper connection to her now .... having experienced her inner realms, it feels like you know her more, you understand some of the trauma she has been processing for us .... you understand that Mother Earth has her own soul, her own contract as our planet ... that we are all one, we are all interconnected, we are all on this journey together .... we are one ...... so the birds are celebrating .... they are singing, rejoicing in the healing that has taken place ... perhaps you can sense the Olani celebrating beneath you! .... suddenly you are surrounded by golden butterflies, they flutter and dance all around you caressing your cheek, landing on you momentarily, thanking you .... and just as suddenly fly away ...... they just came to give you a divine thank you .... and so very very gently, start to bring your awareness back to the room, take a lovely soft deep breath ... still feeling that inner light ... that you know you can shine wherever it is needed ... and opening your eyes whenever you are ready just taking your time.

The Lenali Portals – Creating energy portals for healing the cetacean nation, yourself and your animals

Once again making yourself comfortable take three lovely long deep breaths ...., breathing with the ocean ..... breathing in the golden light, breathing out the golden light ... feeling our inner golden light expanding .... and imagine once again that you're floating on top of this beautiful water ...... in this fabulous ocean and as you look down through the surface of the water, you see all these beautiful lights sparkling, twinkling beneath you .... and you're curious as to where all these lights are coming from? ...... and then the more you look, the more you see, as you gaze downwards ... you see something creating form, something becoming form, whereas before there were just lights and you realise that you are floating above a huge plasma ship, a plasma ship full of healing energy and the ship is kind of undulating very softly beneath you and you feel nothing but love and gentleness emanating from the plasma ship ... as it rises up ... you realise that the energies and frequencies of the beings of this ship, are inviting you to choose whether you would like to enter or whether you would like to just observe ... and the whale mother Lenali comes close just to support you, just to reassure you, and to explain to you that this plasma ship is a place of healing ... for all the whales, all the cetaceans, that have suffered the effects of pollution, the effects of humankind and that they can flow into the plasma ship to be cleansed, to be strengthened, to be re-energised ... and so imagine this immense ship allowing the whales to swim through and you can watch them either inside or outside, whatever feels right for you, but see all the whales and their babies, entering through the plasma walls of the ship and the more whales that come in, this beautiful lavender light, seems to grow more and more inside the plasma ship and as the whales progress through the ship, you can see the lavender light cleansing their auras, washing them clean of stress, any emotional or physical pain, and when they feel able to swim out the other side, they can feel renewed strengthened, supported, for these immense whale beings hold the knowledge of our earth, they hold the knowledge of humankind, they need our help and they need our support and Lenali is the ambassador of the whales and she asks us to visualise all the oceans around the world of our beloved blue planet, and with our prayers, our hearts and our minds, creating more and more healing portals and plasma ships, for the whales to receive that support, that succour, that healing, that cleansing and renewing, so in whatever way you can imagine seeing all the whales, dolphins and sea creatures benefiting from these places of safety, of healing of regeneration, and you think of all the overfishing and the desecration, all the sharks that are slaughtered for their fins, all the turtles, even the coral reefs. Imagine them all to be wrapped in the lavender light of the plasma ships, for the oceans are our life blood, we are the blue planet … and if the oceans die, then so do we ……………………… so rejoice in seeing the whales being able to just rest … release and renew …… and know that this is a place that you may visit, the whales invite you to also receive healing, peace, release, and renewal, and it's a place where you can take other people, other animals, that need that healing release, you can take them with you so they may also receive the healing and renewal. So Lenali thanks you, the whale nation thanks you, the cosmic whales thank you, the golden dolphins thank you … all the sea creatures thank you … every molecule of the ocean thanks you … thank you! … so be it and so it is! …. and so gently bringing your awareness back …. taking a deep breath, just gently bringing yourself back to the room and opening your eyes whenever you are ready.

Healing and reprogramming past, present and future DNA with the Whale Mother Nazkaa

DNA Healing with the divine feminine
2.9 megahertz frequency
Gifted from the Whale Mother Nazkaa activations

Making yourself comfortable, feeling your feet or your body, firmly on the floor, being aware of any chattery thoughts that invade your mind… just send them on their way …. and any sounds outside your room … just allow them to float in and float out and in fact, help you relax even more … focussing on your breath … notice the cool air as you breathe in … and the warmer air as you breathe out …. Start by taking a lovely deep breath in and exhale with a wonderful long loud sigh … letting go of any tension … giving yourself permission to just let go ….. each time you breathe out, feel your body just   surrendering to peace … breathing in peace … breathing out tension …. breathing in peace … breathing out tension … breathing in peace … breathing out love …. breathing in peace … breathing out love … breathing in love … breathing out love … allow all the ocean energies to flow all around you and through you … feel yourself anchored in the ocean energy now …… the energy of our beautiful blue planet ………. call in the great whale mother Nazkaa ………… call in her divine presence ….. breathe in her energy … breathe out her energy …………. breathing in her sound … breathing out her sound …………… allow her to flow into you with the utmost love, compassion, protection …………………………………………… and as her energy flows through your body …… imagine your human overcoat – your outer layers, your human garment … just gently falling away and get a sense of your soul and your inner core being …… your blueprint ……… and as you can sense that ……. as Nazkaa's sound frequencies vibrate through your body, as though facilitating a separation, a peeling away of the old you. Imagine you can leave your human body ……… and with Nazkaa's help you can rise up through time and space … rise up into time between time …………. and imagine that you are held

157

in the most beautiful golden pillar of light .... and this pillar of light is encircled by an immense oval crystal ring and with the loving vibration of the divine feminine, the 2.9 megahertz transmitted by Nazkaa .... the crystal ring is activated and starts to glow with the colour filaments of gold and silver and pink and blue and somehow you can imagine your DNA held lovingly within this golden pillar of light .... and you can observe and be it at the same time .... so observe how the strands of your DNA look, are the strands in balance ..... Are they flowing? Maybe there are some areas that look dark? maybe they are not flowing in harmony ... or synchronised with each other – maybe they seem stuck or not rotating ... Perhaps jamming? What do they look or feel like? .... with the 2.9 frequency, Nazkaa starts to rotate the pillar of light and the centrifugal force very gently starts to bring things into balance .... so observe your DNA being reprogrammed, rebalanced, strengthened, and if you so wish, overlaid within this could be your future incarnations – so maybe observe what your future DNA might look like – maybe you would like to choose a beautiful harmonious, gentle loving healthy future incarnation? It might not be a solid physical incarnation ...... but your soul blue print may still benefit from some balance and healing .... so in whatever way feels right for you allow Nazkaa to bring this balance – this harmony... this unity, into your core DNA.......................
so notice the changes .... notice what is being released ... as the gentle centrifugal force spins your DNA round and round .... anything less than positive is instantly transmuted to the golden light - perhaps you can visualise dark blocked energy spinning away - perhaps you now see the strands becoming more golden? .... just do whatever feels right for you .... you may get a sense of past incarnations, where you may see or feel imbalances – you may call in the DNA from your past and release any toxins from those times .... just observe anything that might need releasing or rebalancing .... knowing that our thoughts and our choices create our realities .... so choose beautiful loving and

harmonious realities .... sending love to all the challenges that you may have endured or undergone .... of all that you have learnt .... feel Nazkaa guiding you now, and these have created who you are now .... and know that every strand now has been encoded with the golden light of the divine feminine frequencies, bringing balance to the masculine ... and just for now allow Nazkaa to gently bring them back down through time and space .... in the time between time .... down into the here and now .... reconnecting with your human garment, your body, this vehicle that allows you to be on earth at this momentous time.......... just allow everything to be reconnected, to be reabsorbed .... allow Nazkaa's sounds to bring you back .... celebrating the healing that has taken place .... she thanks you for your courage ... she honours you for your bravery .... choosing your soul path ... your soul journey .... as she envelops you in her love .... So then just allow her to gently place you back in your chair .... just integrating the crystalline golden energy frequencies into your being .... and very, very gently start to bring your awareness back .... knowing you can take other people, animals... situations... into the golden light with the help of Nazkaa – beautiful Nazkaa, anytime you wish .... she sends you her deepest gratitude and her deepest love .... so taking a nice deep breath .... Opening your eyes whenever you are ready .... taking your time to fully integrate all the healing that has taken place, being very gentle with yourself... opening your eyes whenever you are ready.

The Return of Nagwal

The Golden Diamond Light Code Activation

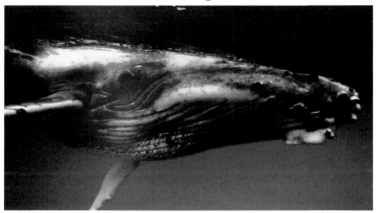

Start by making yourself comfortable either sitting or lying down .... closing your eyes ... and taking three lovely long deep breaths .... all the way in and all the way out ... feel that gentle rise as you breathe in and gentle fall as you breathe out .... Allow any busy thoughts and mind chatter to just float in and then float out - you can deal with them all later, but just for now this is your special time just for you. Give yourself permission to just BE and with each out breath you can say to yourself "The next time I breathe out I can relax even more ... the next time I breathe out, I can relax even more" and notice how beautifully your body responds as each time you breathe out, you feel your shoulders dropping a little more and you can allow yourself to sink down and down ... into your beautiful place of knowing, deep inside of you .... know that you are completely safe and very much loved. The great whales, the ancient whale beings, come now to wrap you in their love. Together you set the intention of allowing deep healing to take place, re-aligning, re-empowering, recalibrating and reconnecting with all that is ... Feel their vibration all around you .... these are the great cosmic whales that join you here today so imagine that you are floating in the most beautiful blue lagoon .... you are very, very safe .... you are completely protected by the whales ....

you find yourself just floating effortlessly .... and feeling waves of love coming from the whales .... coming to you with so much compassion ..... overwhelmingly beautiful ... and you start to feel a vibration in your heart ... it's as though your whole body begins to tingle .... and swimming towards you very softly, very gently, is this wonderful baby whale .... he comes with so much gentleness ... slowly at first ...... so you get used to the energy of this being, so close to you – he just gently swims around you, filling you with his love and you feel his name Nagwal, resonate deep within you .... he is the golden master avatar, who has returned now after eons of time .... he returns into the physical now to co-create this shift, to bring you his love and to activate your heart to align with the new earth .... every cell of your body is now filled with his love ....and when he feels that you are relaxed and feeling safe with his presence ..... he comes so close to you looking into your eyes looking into the very depths of your soul ....
and then you see a golden tear fall from his eye. Within this golden tear is all the pain of the world ... all grief, all sadness of the destruction that has taken place on this our earth ... more golden tears fall, releasing all fear and suffering ....
then he seems to be crying tears of pink and his whole body seems to be releasing pink unconditional love energy ... that feels as though it's filling you with love and the forgiveness for humankind and then you feel the connection with his heart with your heart .... and very softly and very gently, he places the tip of his pectoral fin onto your third eye ..... and with the gentlest of touches, he seems to cause an explosion of synapses in your brain, in the gentlest of ways. Creating new circuits of awareness as these new circuits spark ... connect ..... and fire and in this frozen moment in time ...... you have this huge download of knowing .... and then he moves his fin and touches your heart .... softly gifting you with an incredible golden diamond shaped heart crystal. It somehow seems to just become your heart .... and you feel your diamond crystal changing .... Expanding ..... Resonating .... Activating .... and the energy is flowing through your whole

body ….. as though every cell of your body can have its own dia-
mond crystal and encoded golden light ……… bringing health
………. Healing ………. Joy …. Peace ………   abundance
and most of all so much love ……………………………………
so really feel that golden heart energy in every cell of your body
……. as your hearts unite … awakening your sacred heart now
with the golden   avatar Nagwal ………. he gives you free ac-
cess to the Akashic records- the whales call them the libraries of
love   …..   the   libraries   of   love
…………………………………………….. so if you feel you would
like to travel with him into the libraries of love – let him guide
you now … perhaps there is something you wish to learn about
yourself – about your future self, or maybe about your past jour-
ney with him now ……………………… and know that you can
revisit the libraries of love whenever you wish … but just for
now, allow Nagwal to gently bring you back to the lagoon …
wrapped in his love ………………. as you thank him … and say
farewell, thank all the beautiful whales, who have held the space
for this incredible re-connection, release and   recalibration
…………………. and you find yourself just   climbing out onto
the shore… being wrapped in a lovely soft fluffy towel ………
hearing the sound of the whales as they blow and swim gently
away …………………… you feel when you are wrapped in this
towel, that it is somehow anchoring in all the wonderful golden
light deep within you ……… so imagine you are very gently
being lifted back now and softly being placed in your bed, or
your chair …… wrapped in your beautiful towel ………..
wrapped in love …… filled with the golden light ………. and
just taking your time absorbing and assimilating all your experi-
ences ……….. absorbing and assimilating all the golden light,
and when you feel you have absorbed this light, bring it back
……. So that you can continue to heal, transform and resonate
with the vibrations, frequencies and light codes of the new earth
paradigm……….. and then very, very gently bringing yourself
back to the here and now………. opening your eyes whenever
you are ready, taking a deep breath…… bring yourself back.

Journey into the Golden City with the Golden Dolphins

Eb32h speaks again *"The planetary cognisant are recalibrating the forces of dark energy, utilising the tertiary triangulation points, fusing dark matter through fractal time.... all is ebb and flow of motion!"*

Dante a golden dolphin emissary off Kona Hawaii big Island, told me this...

"The golden orb aligns the 19.5 Latitude crystal structures and grids, put in place, activating and connecting further myceliums also resonating with other outer planetary grids that are now crystallizing and creating new light forces/ frequencies. Our earth is fundamentally changing its vibration in alignment with new galaxies yet to be discovered"

Whilst swimming with the wild spinner dolphins off Ho'okena bay in Hawaii Kona Big Island, I had an amazing experience, as though transported down the spirals of vortex-like light, pouring down through the water into the depths below. The dolphins who were all around me, seemed to encourage me to follow them down and they showed me this huge orb, covered in a silty slime. I felt compelled to try and clear it. Although I knew I was just visualising this – I felt as though I had slipped into another dimension, as I worked with the dolphins, who appeared golden, and other sea creatures to cleanse the orb. After being given this vision, and completing my task, I seemed to bob back into my body, much to the relief of my friends, who had been frantically searching for me, as I had seemed to disappear completely, and couldn't be found either in the water or the beach. They said I had just vanished and then just as suddenly reappeared! This is the meditation given to me from this other dimensional experience!

Healing the Inner Earth and the Emergence of the Golden City

With the Golden Dolphins, Sea Dragons and Narwhals

Find a soft, safe space, either sitting or lying down .... take three lovely longs breaths, feeling the gentle rise as you breathe all the way in .... and the gentle fall as you breathe all the way out .... each time you breathe out, allow your shoulders to drop a little more and give yourself permission to just be! .... imagine that you are floating in the most beautiful crystal turquoise water, with the brilliant sun's rays shining through. The rays shine and spiral downwards into and towards a vanishing point, like a funnel, or creating a vortex of light .... you feel drawn somehow, called, to explore deep into the vortex. You feel no fear and find to your amazement, that you can breathe easily! You feel guided to call in the golden dolphins, who are here now from the higher dimensions to facilitate the ascension of our earth. The golden dolphins come to assist, guiding you, allowing you to journey down into the vortex of light. The dolphins guide you down and down, until you see an enormous orb and you can just make out that inside the orb, is a beautiful golden city. However, the outer surface of the orb seems a little opaque and you feel drawn to wipe away the silt and seaweed-like slime that appears to sully it. You then find that the outer layer is like a strong glutinous kind of membrane, which needs to be broken in order for the golden city to be shining fully in the light and 'unveiled'. Although the dolphins assist you in the cleansing of the orb, they

cannot penetrate the membrane and reveal the golden city. So the leafy sea dragons come in their true form and use their dragon fire to melt away the membrane. The blue eyed white Narwhal Frielaas .... the unicorn of the sea, also comes to assist the piercing of the membrane with his golden horn, to reveal the city in all its glory and beauty, dazzling the eye and free-ing it from constraints and allowing the energy to flow, transmitting and receiving! ....
Now that the brilliance of the city shines up to you, you ask permission to journey down into the city and the healing golden temples therein. You sense that there is someone very special waiting there to thank you and to guide you forwards in your healing journey and how to be of further service to Mother Earth ..... so allow yourself to journey down now, guided by Frielaas, pointing the way with his horn............ In one of the beautiful temples, you meet a being that tells you that it is your infinite self - the 'you' that knows all the answers to all your questions ... ask your infinite, limitless self, how you can go forwards with all the emotional and physical healing and health that you are worthy of and truly deserve right now in your life .... allow your infinite self to guide you. You also ask what Mother Earth needs for you to help her even more. Listen to the guidance now.................... knowing that you can now visit the golden city and your infinite self whenever you wish, but for now, it is time to thank them for their wisdom and guidance that you can store in your heart...... Call the golden dolphins to guide you back now to the surface... up and up ... through the vortex of

light, back to the surface, still bathed in the golden light of the city .... imagine yourself filled with the golden light - every cell of your body shining ... swim back to shore, bringing the golden light with you and rest a while on the cool sand or rocks .... allowing you to absorb and assimilate all your experiences .... When you feel you have integrated all the guidance and healing, gently bring yourself back to the room, rubbing the palms of your hands together until they feel nice and warm and tingly ..... When they feel warm, place them over your eyes and breathe in the warmth .... and then placing your hands back in your lap, taking a nice deep breath and opening your eyes whenever you are ready!

The gift of Sha'ila the white Elephant

Imagine yourself, surrounded by the most beautiful beings - the Elohim, sending their angelic healing light into you ... suddenly the circle parts and the most beautiful white, painted elephant enters and she walks right up to you. You can feel the earth shudder beneath her heavy footfall. She gently touches your

third eye with her bristly trunk, as though assessing your abilities and activating your intuition even more. She then seems to caress your heart centre and then gently places a huge ruby crystal into your etheric heart. She wishes you to remember and recognise your divinity, deep within you. You feel drawn to lean your third eye against her trunk, thanking her for her gift, which you know will imbue you with even more empathy, compassion and love for others, being more able to intuit their needs, which you will be able to assist them with for their highest good, but also knowing that you have been truly blessed by this sacred ambassador of ascension. When she has finished gifting you and you feel that she has received your thanks, she turns and walks away; again you feel the vibration of the earth's tremor, as her huge body sways away, back through the circle of Elohim, who then close the circle once more, facilitating the anchoring of Sha'ila's gift to you, as you rest now absorbing and assimilating your experience.

The lion pyramid portals

The beautiful lion Eddie AKA Aslan, who I met in South Africa, gifted me with this meditation, which has been found to be incredibly powerful, facilitating huge release of negative vibration and blocked energies.

Making yourself comfortable and allowing your breathing to become soft and deep, gently sinking into the safe space of knowing deep within you .... imagine the immense lion being that is Aslan come forwards to you now. Seeing his beautiful face with his deep penetrating eyes, ask Aslan now to guide you through the door of a golden pyramid ..... once inside the pyramid, visualise it filled with golden healing light. This is a healing chamber of golden light. Imagine sitting cross legged, but as though the golden light and the love from Aslan, can levitate you slightly. Once in position, Aslan leaves you there, but you know that his energy is fully supporting you and the healing that will take place now. Imagine yourself slowly rotating anticlockwise, slowly at first, then speeding up to a rate that you are comfortable with. Imagine as you are spinning, that everything that no longer serves you, or is blocking you, can be gently spun out of you. See the blocks and negativity, in whatever way you can imagine them, be transmuted by the golden light as they spin out and away from your body. If you visualise dark energy coming out of you, see it change into beautiful golden raindrops, falling to the ground and creating even more golden light. When you feel that everything that needs to be released has been cleansed today, you can softly allow your body to spin in the opposite direction. In this way you can now fill all the spaces that have been cleared with the golden light, which can somehow be spun into you. Filling your auric light bodies with so much golden light- the more you spin, the more golden you become. Visualise any areas of physical or emotional pain being filled with the golden light. Keep going until you feel you are filled to the brim and the spinning ceases. Just rest on the floor of the pyramid for a few moments, absorbing and assimilating, all the release and all the golden light now filling your body ..... Aslan will know when this has occurred and he now re-enters the pyramid to lead you out. Feel his soft fur as you rest your hand on his back, thanking him for his guidance. Then very gently with no rush, bring yourself back to your room and open your eyes whenever you are ready.

Meeting the golden Unicorns

One evening for my birthday treat, I went to a sound bath, given by a wonderful man called Sika. During the amazing meditative state that the sounds he played created, I imagined sitting by a pool in a magical forest and called in the golden unicorns ... I gazed into the water and suddenly saw their reflections, smiling next to me. I kept looking into the water and telepathically asked them questions about my life's path, I asked ... "Where am I meant to be?" ... When I asked this question, I was told "You are meant to be everywhere! Your dreams about being on stage and not remembering your words to your songs, are telling you that you have a new 'song' to sing, now you are not on stage to sing any more - you are on stage to 'speak' the animals' wisdom!".   I have had several recurring nightmares about being on stage with a big audience waiting to hear my songs, but I couldn't remember any of the words I had written and performed previously.

I would wake up distressed, as I could see the whole audience waiting expectantly and none of my words would come. Now I am asked sometimes to speak at animal conferences, and once I overcome my nerves, the animals start to speak through me and now I find it hard to stop!! So see if the unicorns can answer some of your questions!!!

Close your eyes … after taking some wonderful deep breaths - giving yourself permission to just let go … imagine sitting by a pool in a magical forest and call in the golden unicorns… as you gaze into the water you will see their reflections, smiling next to you. Just keep looking into the water and telepathically ask them any questions you wish to ask about your life's path. Listen carefully to their guidance asking for more clarity if needed. When you have received an answer to your questions, perhaps they may touch you with their golden horns, or by touching the water, it will turn gold and you may choose to bathe in it, receiving more healing energy from them ….. when you have finished ….. thank your golden friends, and bring yourself gently back to the room, bringing back all the wonderful messages and healing from the unicorns.

The crystal vault of source

Mweti, the beautiful white lioness, kept appearing as a vision in the doorway of my office. This continued for about a week and I knew that she wanted me to do something, but for a while I could not understand what she wanted. Then suddenly she said to me … "You have to go to the crystal vault!" Ok I thought, what happens next? She said that she would give me a key and that my friend Charlotte also needed one, so that we could unlock the vault together simultaneously. So that night I asked Mweti to give us our keys. Mine seemed to me, like a crystal in the shape and form of something like a Tudor Rose, which would sit inside a similar shape that could then be turned. I arranged for Charlotte to visualise doing this with me, with her key that she had intuited being gift-ed by Mweti. I asked Mweti what would be contained within the crystal vault and she said it was even more than the Akashic records- it was the most sacred place. I couldn't imagine anywhere having more information or power than the Akashic records, but of course I wasn't going to doubt her! I had previously just undergone a powerful initiation, in a workshop with a wonderful man called Divyael, where he had led us through a cleansing violet fire. I had visualised walking through several very thick golden doors, that kept opening for me and then finally, I was in this huge cavern, where the violet fire burned. I felt that I had to guide Charlotte through all the golden doors and then through the fire and then I somehow knew that the door to the crystal vault would be on the other side. So she went through all the doors and the violet fire, and then we both imagined standing in front of the huge vault door. Simultaneously we placed our keys in the appropriate opening or 'slot', and imagined turning them. The huge, immensely thick door opened, rather like a bank vault. Once inside, we could both see lots of the most beautiful golden crystals, in the most gorgeous shapes. The energy in there was overwhelmingly beautiful. We stood inside and felt nothing but the purest form of love and Mweti said we were in the vault of pure source, containing the most powerful force of all... LOVE! It felt so amazing, as we were filled with the golden crystal light, giving us the deepest feeling of peace we had ever felt. So maybe you would like to experience this for yourself!

Close your eyes, take some lovely deep breaths... all the way in and all the way out… and with each out breath allow yourself to just let go more and more… any chattery thoughts that come into your mind, just send them on their way, you can deal with them all later, but just for now this is your special time, to just be…… When you are ready imagine you are standing in front of a huge golden door. Imagine sending love from your heart into the door, which then seems to develop an image of a heart growing in the gold of the door. By increasing the heart centred energy from your heart….. the force is so strong that the door begins to open inwards and you can walk through… after a few steps you find another big golden door in front of you… again you set the intention of sending your heart energy towards it, asking to be allowed to enter through the doorway and to your amazement the door swings slowly inwards allowing you through. The passage way you are in is very well lit and you can notice the surface of the ground you are walking on and the walls along this passageway….. You then come to one more door and as you send your loving energy once more… the words "Your Infinite Self" seem to magically appear upon the door… once you see the words, you know that your infinite self will be guiding you to reconnect with the source of all that is and the only true power of all….. The door opens into a large cavern and within the cavern is a large fire, burning a violet flame…. although you may feel a little wary at first, just know that you are so loved by your infinite self and no harm can befall you. You feel guided to summon up your courage, knowing that you are completely safe, and walk into the fire, standing in the centre of the violet flames…. You feel cleansed and somehow lighter by the flames…when you step out of the fire you will see the huge door to the crystal vault. Now that it has been opened once more, by the crystal keys, it is not locked and you can enter at will…. When you go inside you are momentarily dazzled by the golden hue of the crystals within… stand amongst the crystals and experience the downloading and absorption of the pure love, which fills your being. You can stay here for as long as you like and know that you can place people and animals within the vault who may need the healing of the golden love crystals. It is a place of immense power which should be revered and honoured. When you are ready to leave, give thanks for all the healing love that you have received, knowing that you can return at any time either for yourself or to accompany another who may be in need, but just for now close the door behind you... The cleaning violet fire seems to have disappeared for now and you can walk back through the open doors, through the passageway. As you pass through the golden doors, they close slowly behind you. As you turn and face the last golden door, on the outside of it you can just see the image of the heart within the surface of the door.... With the utmost respect, you send so much gratitude to your higher self and the crystals, whose resonance and vibratory frequencies still remain within you.... Then taking another deep breath... gently start to bring your awareness back to the room... opening your eyes whenever you are ready.

Conclusion

How can you find unity?

I think you'll agree that the case studies and wild encounters that you've read about have shown just how incredible the animal kingdom and nature realms are. I feel that their knowledge of what we need to heal is far superior to ours! I regularly feel as though we are playing catch up to the wisdom of our animals, who know so much about us. The cases in part one, were, for me, mind blowing in the healing potential that the humans had, to embrace their lives and release their pain both physically and emotionally.

There are so many gifts in this book, so many messages of hope and guidance for all of us. I am constantly humbled by the willingness of these multi-dimensional beings to share their healing frequencies with us. To be guided as to how to re-programme our very DNA and re-write our soul contracts. To journey back in time to heal the past, to fly to alternative universes, to be able to delve deep within ourselves, to bring out the best we can be, to fulfil our potentials and make our dreams our realities for a heaven on earth.

If we can open our hearts and mind we can achieve this! By working with the techniques shared by the animals in this book, we can really unify - uniting for a wondrous future, completely connected with our beloved Mother Earth.

So I truly hope that you can find something for you in this book to guide you forwards and assist you in honouring both yourself and of course the animals that you are lucky enough to have with you at this momentous time!

Here is a message about Ascension from the great white whale mother!

The White Whale Unity and Ascension

"With the guidance of the great white whale, I release all fear, worry, guilt and doubt from my being now! - With the guidance of the great white whale I embrace only love, courage, forgiveness and belief into my being now!"

This is a mantra given to me by the great white whale mother - she came to me one night like a huge mother ship, as she seemed to hover over me, asking me to spread my arms and legs like a star and imagine her touching my fingers with the huge white fins, downloading the white whale unity consciousness energies into me, as I repeated the mantra. It was such an incredible experience and she asks that you allow her to come to you now. She says that she chooses you, because you are ready for her message and download of energies!

So allow her to come to you to be filled with the unity consciousness and see how she can facilitate your spirit to be renewed and your passion restored. If you feel downhearted or diminished, call her in. When communicating with her and asking her about the white whale consciousness, she said;

"it is a collective of the highest and purest of the whale and dolphin consciousness. You might say it comes from the masters of cetacean masters. It is a very high loving vibration and tapping into this is very helpful for all beings."

I asked her how can we connect to it and use it. Her answer was;

"You connect to it like you do to anything else. Sit quietly, open your heart, call out mentally, use your intention to connect with it, and wait. Nothing new and different to make the connection, but the important part is to hold that energy. Let it wash into your body and soul, bathe yourself in it and allow it to flow into each and every cell. This high energy has the capacity to heal you on many levels, so allow it to do just that. You can work with it daily if you like for your own good or the planet. Once

174

Acknowledgements

This book has taken four years to come into fruition. So many publishing companies turned it down, because they felt that the message was too arcane, too niche. That maybe so, but my mission has been to share this message for all who are open minded and open hearted enough to receive it.

I'd like to thank Samantha Curtis. A wonderful agent, who tried tirelessly to find a MBS publisher for me, I know she believed in the power and importance of this book.

However I feel now that with the help of Lynn Morris of Evolution of the Soul Publishing, that my book and I have come home. *Finally*, I get the chance to fulfil my mission, given to me by the animals. I can't wait to see how the ripple effects created by the reading of this book, begin to raise the vibration of the human consciousness and awareness. There is so much magic available to us, if we are brave enough to grasp it. So I am forever indebted to Lynn for taking this book on when no-one else would!

I would also like to thank my dear friend Nori Neumann for allowing me to use her artwork "Bright Future" for the cover, which to me encapsulates the support and healing of humankind, surrounded by the cetaceans and the animal kingdom. Her other beautiful paintings that she generously allowed me to include within the book, enhance it even further. Big thank you to Jenny Smedley for her constant support and motivation to start writing all those years ago and to Marta Williams for her kind endorsement; she is a truly great ambassador for animal communication and ecological awareness. also Lisa Tenzin Dolma, who works tirelessly raising awareness and understanding of the psychology of dogs, and also her beautiful books, who have graced bookstores for many years, especially her fabulous book "Charlie the dog who came in from the wild". It is a real honour to receive such a beautiful endorsement from her. Huge thankyou also to Dr Linda Bender for her support and her courageous work in animal conservation and protection. It was so much fun meeting you and sharing experiences with Credo, Izak and of course the royal pride of star lions.

I'd also like to thank Leon Smith from Vula Tours in South Africa, for giving me the most incredible experiences and introducing me to Adam's Calendar. I also like to thank Andrew and Diane Clarke from Vaka Vave Charter for facilitating the most awe inspiring encounters with the whales off Vava'u, Kingdom of Tonga.

I'd love to thank Anne Gordon for allowing me to join her to co-facilitate our beautiful whale and dolphin retreat, sailing around the astonishingly beautiful Pearl Islands of Panama, where I connected with the white whale consciousness. She was also co-founder of the Cetacean Summit and she kindly invited me to speak at the summit on Kona big island Hawaii and Dana Point California - she also took me by boat, deep into the Panamanian jungle to meet her friends the people of the Embera tribe... how lucky was I!

Huge hugs to my wonderful friend Khomani San bushman shaman Izak Kruiper - I am forever in love with your gentle energy and the iconic Credo Mutwa, who gave me my Zulu name and generously spent time with us, allowing us to also share meals with him and his family. His contribution to raising awareness of consciousness for the planet is immeasurable. Big thanks to Mbali Creso for facilitating these meetings.

Huge thanks to all the people who agreed to allow me to share their stories in Part One, illustrating the incredible healing shifts that took place with the help of their furry friends!

Finally a big thank you to the wonderful members of my

family and friends who looked after my youngest son and my animals, whilst I was off having adventures, gleaning the information in this book- you are so appreciated and I would not have been able to globe trot without your help!

Bibliography

Children of the Sun God by Linda Tucker

Saving the White Lions by Linda Tucker

Adam's Calendar: The Seventy Great Mysteries of the Ancient World: Discovering the Oldest Man-made Structure on Earth by John Heine and Michael Tellinger

Your Souls Plan by Robert Schwartz

The Whale Whisperer by Madeleine Walker

An Exchange of Love by Madeleine Walker

Dolphins and Whales Forever by Takara Shellor et al (collaboration)

Animal Wisdom - Learning from the Spiritual Lives of Animals by Linda Bender

Resources

www.artbynori.org
www.emberavillagetours.com
www.evolutionofselfpublishing.com
www.healingorchids.com
www.horsebacktrails.co.za
www.jennysmedley.co.uk
www.lindabender.org
www.vulatours.co.za
www.martawilliams.com
www.mettaart.com
www.theiscp.com
www.whalewatchingpanama.com
www.whalewatchswimtonga.com
www.whitelions.org

About the Author

Madeleine Walker is a world renowned Animal Communicator, Horse and Rider Trauma Consultant and Spiritual Empowerment Coach. Her mission is to raise humankind's awareness of the incredibly deep connections we have with our animals, and the importance now of their messages of healing re-empowerment for us and our beautiful planet. She travels extensively to work with wild species, e.g. lions, elephants, whale sharks and large cetaceans, in their natural habitat, and writes and lectures internationally, about her experiences. She is well known for her healing skills for both animals and humans on both emotional and physical levels. Madeleine specializes in the past life connections between animals and their human carers. She is a pioneer with her ground breaking techniques on past life script rewriting, cetacean soul healing and pre-birth soul contract realigning, all taught to her by animals! She formerly worked in adult education with holistic stress management and Art therapy and also worked within conventional veterinary medicine. She is based in the UK, but facilitates courses internationally. She also performs distant consultations for her overseas client base. She has been featured on many US (including Coast to Coast), Canadian, and Australian, radio shows, and in many international publications. She was also a finalist in the 2013 About.com reader's choice awards for favourite Animal Communicator, and her "Animal Whispers Empowerment cards" were also nominated as finalists in the favourite Oracle card set category. She has written three books, her first book "An Exchange of Love ... Animals healing people in past, present and future lifetimes" published by O Books. "The Whale Whisperer" and "Your Pets' Past Lives and how they can heal you" (now translated into Chinese and German) published by Findhorn Press.

Her meditation CDs "Whale Whispers, Lion Roars - a journey to re-empowerment" channelled meditations from the whales and sacred white lions, "Fearless Earth meditations for Gaia" and "Whale Hearts and Dragon Flight... Gifts from the Guardians of Gaia" also her Oracle card set "Animal Whispers Empowerment Cards" are also available from Findhorn press and Amazon etc.... and now the "Guardians of Gaia Earth Keeper Oracle Cards with Whales and Dragons" available from Madeleine's Website www.madeleinewalker.co.uk and Amazon and on www.evolutionofselfpublishing.com.

Published by Evolution of Self Publishing House
Copyright 2017 ©
www.evolutionofselfpublishing.com

Lightning Source UK Ltd.
Milton Keynes UK
UKOW07f1811120517

301083UK00013B/59/P